THE
ULTIMATE

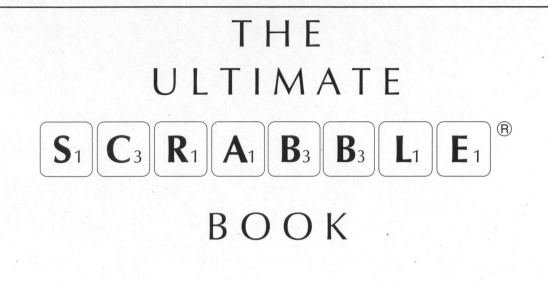

BOOK

THE
ULTIMATE

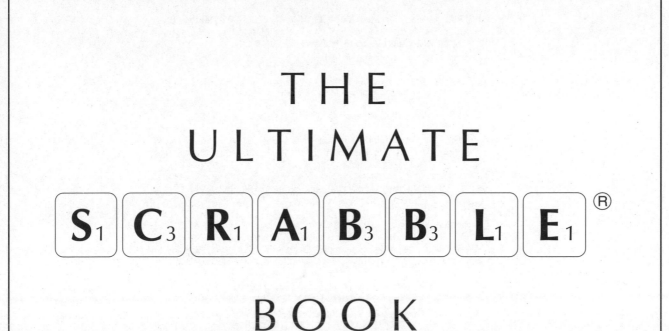

BOOK

Philip Nelkon

STANLEY PAUL
LONDON

3 5 7 9 10 8 6 4 2

First published 1995

© Complete Editions Ltd and J.W. Spear & Sons PLC, 1995

Philip Nelkon, Complete Editions Ltd and J. W. Spear & Sons PLC have asserted their right under the Copyright, Designs and Patent Act, 1988 to be identified as the authors of this work

First published in the United Kingdom in 1995 by
Stanley Paul

Random House, 20 Vauxhall Bridge Road, London SW1V 2SA
Random House Australia (Pty) Limited
20 Alfred Street, Milsons Point, Sydney, New South Wales 2061, Australia
Random House New Zealand Limited, 18 Poland Road, Glenfield, Auckland 10, New Zealand
Random House South Africa (Pty) Limited
PO Box 337, Bergvlei, South Africa
Random House UK Limited Reg. No. 954009

A CIP catalogue record for this book is available from the British Library

ISBN 0091810140

Designed by Craig Dodd

Typeset by Michael Mepham, Frome, Somerset
Printed and bound in Great Britain by
Butler & Tanner Ltd, Frome, Somerset

CONTENTS

S
C
R
A
B
B
L
E

ACKNOWLEDGEMENTS

I am grateful to a significant number of people who have helped in the preparation of this book. In particular I would like to express my thanks to Barry Grossman who helped with the puzzles and the quiz, and to Graeme Thomas for checking those solutions.

Reference is made throughout the book to *Onwords* – The Scrabble Enthusiasts' Magazine, which is described in detail later. Allan Simmons, the editor and publisher, has kindly given permission for a number of articles and other items originally published in *Onwords* to be reproduced here. To him and to the original authors I extend my very sincere thanks. Allan and they are leading figures in the development and playing of Scrabble and, as I hope you will discover, players at all levels can learn a great deal from them.

Scrabble is an international game and Nick Ballard, editor and publisher of the American Scrabble magazine *Medleys*, has also generously given permission for us to reproduce his account of the thrilling fourth game of the 1993 World Scrabble Championship final as well as his own variant of Scrabble which is described later.

The importance to Scrabble of various publications by Chambers will become evident in the pages that follow and the kind permission of Chambers Harrap Publishers Ltd to reproduce word lists and extracts from word lists published in *Official Scrabble Lists* (1995) is gratefully acknowledged.

I would also like to thank the Associated Press Ltd for permission to reproduce the photograph of Alfred Butts, Paul Starr for permission to reproduce photographs from the 1992 National Scrabble Championships and Marty Heitner for permission to reproduce the photograph of Joel Wapnick.

S

C

R

A

B

B

L

E

INTRODUCTION

I owe my very existence to a board game, but it isn't Scrabble. In the winter of 1936 my father, not long down from Oxford and starting out on a career as a London lawyer, visited Selfridge's department store in Oxford Street and bought one of the first sets of Monopoly to be sold in Britain. He took the prized box back to his digs in Gower Street and asked his landlady if she would be interested in playing the game with him. She demurred, but suggested he introduce himself to another of her lodgers, a young lady studying law at London University. My father knocked on the law student's door and invited her to play a game of Monopoly with him. Within a matter of weeks they were married. We take board games seriously in our family.

By the time I was born in 1948, the fourth of my parents' five children, the American crossword game that Alfred Butts had conceived at the start of the 1930s had been developed by James Brunot into the game of Scrabble as we know it. It didn't arrive in the United Kingdom until 1954 but the Brandreths, of course, were among the first to buy a set. At home we played the game on an almost daily basis, but it was at my boarding school, Bedales, that I began to become quite expert.

Bedales, a school where wordsmiths always felt very much at home (the parents ranged from Oscar Wilde to Robert Graves via Richard Spear, the man who brought Scrabble to Europe), was founded in the 1890s by a pioneer of progressive education, John Badley. By the time I arrived at the school, in the early 1960s, Mr Badley was reaching his century and living in quiet retirement in a cottage in the school grounds. On Wednesday afternoons I was one of the pupils invited to take tea with our revered founder and join him in a game of Scrabble. We played many games together and invariably the old man won. He won, a) because he was the better player; b) because he got away with using obsolete words insisting they had been current in his youth; and c) because his housekeeper kept the score and I rather think she may have cooked the books. (As she also cooked the scones, it didn't do to argue.) As time went by my determination to beat Mr Badley grew. I went into serious training, made a determined effort to enlarge my vocabulary, memorized those useful little words that can make all the difference (like yex and jo and xi) and, eventually, just as the great man was entering his one hundred and second year, I beat him by four points! A month later he was dead. As I mentioned, we take board games seriously in our family.

In 1971 I founded the National Scrabble Championships. I did so simply by placing a small advertisement in the Personal Column of *The Times* inviting anyone interested in taking part to drop me a line. Within days, hundreds had. As well as enthusiastic letters from demented Scrabble buffs from north, south, east and west, my voluminous postbag brought a stern missive from the official PR people for Spear's Games enquiring what I thought I was up to. In fact, it was a relief to hear from them because I hadn't reckoned on my innocuous small ad producing such an avalanche of interest. I got together with Spear's, we became firm friends and together established an annual competition that I am proud to say is soon to celebrate its silver jubilee. Today thousands take part in

S
C
R
A
B
B
L
E

the National Scrabble Championships, there's a thriving schools' championship, there's a world championship. In 1995 a Scrabble competition was even at the centre of legal action, there are Scrabble clubs in every corner of the globe, Scrabble on TV, Scrabble T-shirts, Scrabble pens – and, now, at last, *The Ultimate Scrabble Book*.

Philip Nelkon is a brilliant Scrabble player. He has brought together what amounts to a complete gazetteer of the highways and byways of the world's most popular word game. I can't guarantee that reading it will make you as good a player as a true champion like Philip (or our mutual friend Clive Spate who once scored 979 in a two-handed game, including a cool 320 points scored with the one word WALTZING), but I know it will increase your understanding and enjoyment of a truly glorious game that, in my and Mr Badley's experience, not only enriches life but prolongs it. No wonder we take board games seriously in our family.

GYLES BRANDRETH

THE SCRABBLE® STORY

On 8 April 1993 *The Times* along with other national papers carried the news that Alfred Butts, a ninety-three year old resident of Rhinebeck, New York, had died four days earlier.

`Architect of Scrabble dies' ran the heading in *The Times*, neatly punning and defining Butts's life and work. An architect by training, he also drafted the principles of Scrabble in a number of embryonic games. But that was some twenty years before Scrabble as it is played and enjoyed today took the world of word and board games by storm. Alfred Butts may have been the inspiration behind Scrabble, but the work and guidance of others helped shape the game and give the impetus to see it through to the huge success it was to become.

The story of Scrabble dates from the early years of the Great Depression. The downturn in the US economy hit the construction industry hard and Alfred Butts joined the ranks of the unemployed in 1931. From childhood Butts had been keen on anagrams, crosswords and similar puzzles which proliferated in a number of specialist magazines.

With time on his hands he set about devising a word game of his own. A study of existing games revealed three broad categories: games based on numbers, like dice and bingo; games based on moves, like chess and draughts; and word games, which had stimulated Butts's initial interest. More significantly his research of the games' market showed that there were no commercial word games. Out of work and low on funds he could see that a successful word game might make him some money. So he set to work on a game that combined chance and skill as well as reflecting his enthusiasm for anagrams and crosswords.

By 1933 he had roughed out the ideas for a game he called Lexiko. In its earliest version this had letters and racks, but no board. Nor did the tiles carry any point values. The aim of the game was to form the largest seven-letter word with the letters in one's rack. If a player couldn't see a word, tiles could be exchanged for others drawn from the pool of unused ones. This exchange continued until one of the two,

three or four players was able to construct a seven-letter word, so winning the game. Though it was very simple, the game was fun and Alfred Butts was encouraged to develop it.

The next step was to award point values to the different letters of the alphabet. The distribution of the 100 Lexiko letters had been arrived at by reading the front page of the *New York Times* and counting how many times each letter appeared. This small survey gave Butts the basis for the frequency of letters in his set and this letter distribution remains the same in Scrabble today. The point values he assigned to the letters are a different matter. Butts's original point values have long since been forgotten. They may have been the same as those on Scrabble tiles, but there is no way of confirming that.

The importance of the point values was that they introduced a ranking system to Lexiko. Once a player had gone out with a seven-letter word, the remaining players could play four-, five-, or six-letter words. The scores were totted up and the players ranked according to their scores.

In its revised form Lexiko was sufficiently popular among Butts's friends and colleagues for him to be persuaded to offer it to several games manufacturers. None were interested and none had any suggestions on ways of improving the game.

Undeterred, Alfred Butts introduced his own amendments, most notably the board with premium squares. He also dispensed with the seven-letter word finish, replacing it with a system of moves that allowed players to place interlocking words on the board, with a score for each move.

The name changed too and under its radically new guise the game was offered to the commercial games market as It, only for It to be rejected as well.

Over the following years Alfred Butts continued his refinements. He tried a new name, Criss Cross Words this time. He experimented with different positions for the opening word; at one

Alfred Butts in later life with an early version of Scrabble

time it was played near the upper left corner of the board.

Butts continued making sets of the game himself, producing blueprints of the board drawn with his architectural drafting equipment and pasting these onto folding draughts boards. The tiles were produced in the same way from hand-lettered originals, before being glued onto pieces of quarter-inch plywood cut to match the squares on the board.

In 1939 one of the small number of enthusiasts for Butts's game, a social worker named Neva Deardorff, introduced Alfred Butts to Jim Brunot, a fellow social worker whom she thought might give Butts a hand in launching his game commercially. The two men got together and might have got further in promoting the game if World War II hadn't distracted their attention for the next few years.

One attempt was made in 1942 to market Criss Cross Words, but like previous attempts that was unsuccessful and nothing of significance happened again until the war had ended and Brunot and Butts got together once more, again at the urging of Neva Deardorff.

This time serious plans were made to relaunch the game. Jim Brunot and his wife formed the Production and Marketing Company at their home in Newtown, Connecticut, authorized by Alfred Butts to manufacture the game. The Brunots refined and simplified the game, rearranging the premium squares and streamlining the rules. They also needed to protect the game through a unique brand name. From a long list of possibles, including Logo-Loco, Scrabble was the final choice and in 1949 the first sets went on sale.

In a small, vacant schoolhouse in Dodgingtown, Connecticut, the Brunots and a friend produced the sets by hand, stamping letters one at a time on wooden tiles. They managed an output of twelve sets an hour but even this outstripped demand in the first full year of production when 2400 sets were sold, resulting in a loss of $450. In 1950 sales doubled, but the company still made a loss. In spite of another virtual doubling of sales in the third year the company still failed to make any money and the first six months of 1952 didn't look any more promising. Jim Brunot and his wife set off for a trip to Kentucky unaware that their fortunes were about to change radically.

At much the same time Jack Strauss, the chairman of New York's influential department store Macy's, was also on holiday. Standing at the junction of Broadway and West 34th Street, Macy's offered Manhattan shoppers a large range of high-quality and stylish goods; where Macy's led, other stores followed. On holiday Jack Strauss played Scrabble with friends and became hooked. Back behind his office desk he was surprised to discover that Macy's didn't stock Scrabble. A large order to Brunot's company rectified that, backed by a big promotion on the part of the store.

Back from their Kentucky break the Brunots found themselves swamped with orders. From late 1952 and over the next two years 4½ million sets of Scrabble were sold! America went Scrabble crazy. *Readers Digest, Life* and other national magazines ran articles on the new game which rapidly spread right across the country.

The Brunot's soon realized the time had come to step into the big league and they licensed Selchow and Righter, one of the leading games manufacturers, to market and distribute the game in the United States and Canada. The Brunot's Production and Marketing Company retained the rights to manufacture anything but the standard Scrabble set, but Selchow and Righter were happy to have the rights for the manufacture and marketing of the standard game. Such was the success of Scrabble that thirty-five workers churning out 6,000 sets a week couldn't keep up with the demand.

Nobody complained about the success of Scrabble. For three years orders for the game had to be allocated to ensure that everyone could receive their fair share. The Brunots made their fortune but they did not forget

Alfred Butts who received three cents a set and even on that never had to work again.

On the back of its phenomenal American success the game spread overseas. In 1954 J.W. Spear & Sons PLC acquired the distribution rights to Scrabble in Great Britain. Their first year brought in sales of 4½ million sets.

At the same time Scrabble was gaining a firm foothold in Australia.

From then on Scrabble sales continued to grow and expand. In 1969 J.W. Spear & Sons PLC acquired the world-wide rights to the game outside the United States, Canada and Australia. Two years later Selchow & Righter bought the exclusive rights to Scrabble in the USA and Canada. And T.R. Urban and Company, the Australian distributor which had done so much to establish the game there since 1953, acquired the complete Australian rights at the same time. (Today the Australian rights are owned by J.W. Spear & Sons PLC as well.)

Since its launch Scrabble has grown to be the world's leading word game. Over 100 million games have been sold in 120 countries around the world and today Scrabble is produced in thirty-one languages. As well as the standard Scrabble sets, the game is available in the De Luxe version and as a travel version. Junior Scrabble has been developed for young players. There are Braille sets available for visually impaired players.

You can play Scrabble on computer and watch Scrabble on television. There are books by leading exponents teaching advanced play. Authoritative magazines like the UK's *Onwords*, regularly keep Scrabble enthusiasts up to date with developments in the game at home and abroad. As you will read later, the UK National Scrabble Championship has been held since 1971 and twenty years after that the first World Scrabble Championship between top players from twenty countries was held in London.

In spite of this universal success, Alfred Butts remained surprised that people played the game so seriously. His own approach to the success of Scrabble was always relaxed, perhaps because he was never that good a player; ironically poor spelling let him down. In fact Selchow and Righter had no idea about the part he had played in the development of their winning product until 1981 when company officials spotted a newspaper article about him. Alfred Butts hadn't thought to tell them about his role in the development of Scrabble and nor apparently had anyone else.

After the death of his wife, Butts had started work on a new game which Selchow & Righter took up with enthusiasm this time, calling it Alfred's Other Game. At the age of eighty-one Alfred Butts found himself accelerated into the fast lane. Selchow & Righter flew him to Scrabble tournaments around the USA and introduced him to the New York press to promote a Scrabble show on television. `They send what I would call a limousine. Now I know it's called a limo', Butts disarmingly told the *Wall Street Journal*.

His new found status brought other surprises. Selchow & Righter announced that part of its marketing plan for Alfred's Other Game included a picture on the box of the balding octogenarian dressed in a dinner jacket and accompanied by a young brunette in a low-cut dress. `After eighty years of nothing, I'm a celebrity,' said the bemused inventor.

Since then the Milton Bradley Company, the leading game company in the USA, have acquired the North American rights to Scrabble, adding a new DeLuxe Travel SCRABBLE® to the range and a Super SCRABBLE® Gameboy for Nintendo owners.

In July 1994 Mattel Inc., another leading American toy and games company took over J.W. Spear & Sons PLC to encourage the development of Spear's branded products around the world by harnessing Mattel's world-wide distribution network.

Alfred Butts, Jim Brunot, Neva Deardorff, Jack Strauss and all their friends and relatives and the other Scrabble fans who played their part in the development of the game would have smiled to see two of today's foremost games companies eagerly promoting the game which had been so unreservedly rejected in its earlier forms a generation earlier. ❑

RULES OF PLAY

(All the turns illustrated refer to the Guide Game which follows these rules)

To Begin

Turn all tiles face down at the side of the board, or put them into the bag provided, and shuffle. Draw for first play. The player drawing the tile nearest the beginning of the alphabet plays first. Put the exposed tiles back and reshuffle. Each player then draws seven new tiles and places them on his rack.

One player is elected as scorekeeper. He may also take part in the game.

Method of Play

1   The first player combines two or more of his tiles to form a word and places them on the board to read either across or down with one tile on the centre square (star).

In this example the R of Horn is placed on the centre square.

Turn 1 – Score 14

2   A player completes his turn by counting and announcing his score for the turn which is recorded by the scorekeeper (see rule 11). He then draws as many new tiles as he has played, thus always keeping seven tiles in his rack.

3   Play then passes to the left. The second player, then each in turn, adds one or more tiles to those already played so as to form new words.

All tiles played in any one turn must be placed in one row across or down the board. Diagonal words are not permitted. The tiles played must form one complete word and if, at the same time, they touch other tiles in adjacent rows, they must form complete words cross-word fashion, with all such tiles. The player gets full credit for all words formed or modified by his play.

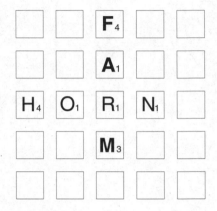

Turn 2 – Score 9

4   **New words** may be formed by:

a)   Adding one or more tiles to a word already on the board.
b)   Placing a word at right angles to a word already on the board. The new word must use one of the letters of the word already on the board or must add a letter to it. It may also `bridge' two or more words.

		F$_4$		
		A$_1$		
H$_4$	O$_1$	R$_1$	N$_1$	
		M$_3$		
P$_3$	A$_1$	S$_1$	T$_1$	E$_1$

Turn 3 - Score 25

Farms	10
Paste	15
Total	25

		F$_4$		
		A$_1$		
H$_4$	O$_1$	R$_1$	N$_1$	
		M$_3$	O$_1$	B$_3$
P$_3$	A$_1$	S$_1$	T$_1$	E$_1$

Turn 4 - Score 16

Mob	8
Not	4
Be	4
Total	16

		F$_4$		
S$_1$		A$_1$		
H$_4$	O$_1$	R$_1$	N$_1$	
O$_1$		M$_3$	O$_1$	B$_3$
P$_3$	A$_1$	S$_1$	T$_1$	E$_1$
S$_1$				

Turn 5 - Score 10

Here is an example of a `bridging' move (see rule 4b)

c) Placing a complete word parallel to a word already played so that adjoining tiles also form complete words.

					H$_4$
				M$_3$	E$_1$
				O$_1$	R$_1$
		F$_4$		D$_2$	O$_1$
		A$_1$		E$_1$	
H$_4$	O$_1$	R$_1$	N$_1$	L$_1$	
		M$_3$	O$_1$	B$_3$	S$_1$

Turn 11 - Score 27

Hero	7
Double Word Score	×2
	14
Me	4
Double Word Score	×2
	8
Or	2
Do	3
Total	27

5 No tile may be shifted after it has been played.

6   The two **blank tiles** may be used as any letter desired. When playing a blank the player must state what letter it represents, after which it cannot be changed during the game.

7   Any player may use his turn to **replace** any or all of the **tiles** in his rack. He does so by discarding them face down, drawing the same number of new tiles, then mixing the discarded tiles with those remaining in the pool. He then awaits his next turn to play.

Instead of placing tiles on the board, or exchanging tiles, a player may also **pass**, whether or not he is able to make a word (or words).

However, should all players pass twice in succession, the game ends.

8   **Permitted Words**: Any words listed in a standard English dictionary are permitted except those only spelt with an initial capital letter, abbreviations, prefixes and suffixes and words requiring apostrophes and hyphens. Foreign words in a standard English dictionary are considered to have been absorbed into the English language and are allowed. Consult a dictionary only to check spelling or usage. Any word may be challenged before the next player starts his turn. If the word challenged is unacceptable, the player takes back his tiles and loses his turn.

9   The **game ends** when all the tiles have been drawn and one of the players has used all the tiles in his rack. The game also ends when all possible plays have been made or all players have passed twice in consecutive turns.

Scoring

10   The scorekeeper keeps tally of each player's score, entering it after each turn on the scorepad. The **score value** of each letter is indicated by a number at the bottom of the tile. The score value of a blank is zero.

11   The score for each turn is the sum of the score values of all the tiles in each word formed or modified in that turn plus the premium values resulting from placing tiles on premium squares.

12   **Premium Letter Squares**: A light blue square doubles the score of a letter placed on it; a dark blue square trebles the letter score.

13   **Premium Word Squares**: The score for the entire word is doubled when one of its tiles is placed on a light red square; it is trebled when a tile is placed on a dark red square. Include premiums for double- or triple-letter values, if any, before doubling or trebling the word score.
     If a word is formed that covers two premium word squares, the score is doubled and then re-doubled (four times letter score), or trebled and then re-trebled (nine times letter score) as the case may be. Note that the centre square (star) is a light red square and therefore doubles the score for the first word.

14   The above letter and word premiums apply only in the turn in which they are first played. In subsequent turns tiles count at face value.

15   When a blank tile falls on a light red or dark red square, the sum of the tiles in the word is doubled or trebled even though the blank itself has no score value.

16   When two or more words are formed in the same turn, each is scored. The common letter is counted (with full premium value, if any) in the score for each word, as in turns 3 and 4 above.

17   Any player who plays all seven of his tiles in a single turn scores a premium of 50 points in addition to his regular score for the turn. The 50 points are added on **after** doubling or tripling a word score, as in Guide Game turn 19.

C₃					
O₁			P₃		
N₁	J₈		R₁		
Q₁₀	U₁	I₁	T₁	E₁	
U₁		G₂		V₄	
E₁				E₁	
S₁			A₁	N₁	
T₁			T₁	H₄	O₁

Turn 19 – Score 212

Conquest	18
Triple Word Score	×3
	54
Triple Word Score	×3
	162
50 bonus points	+50
Total	212

18 At the end of the game each player's score is reduced by the sum of his unplayed tiles, and if one player has used all his tiles, his score is increased by the sum of the unplayed tiles of all the other players.

Some Do's and Don't's

Form words only across the board from left to right or from top to bottom - never diagonally or upwards, as these latter words would not be permissible.

Do not place tiles on the board that result in incomplete or non-existent words. Refer to the Guide Game, turn 11. At this point ADO has not been played, if the player had wished to make HERD instead of HERO, he would have been left with `DD' instead of `DO', which is not permissible.

Words must be separated from each other by a vacant square as in cross-word puzzles, unless both words together form a complete word. Refer to the Guide Game as it appears after turn 26. A player might wish to make GATE beginning with the `G' in LYING. But this would bring the final `E' into contact with LIED. The result would be GATELIED, which is not a word, so that this too would not be permissible.

When one player has used all his tiles and the pool is empty, the game is at an end. No more moves may be made. In some games no player succeeds in using all his tiles. In this case the game continues until all possible moves have been made. If a player is unable to move he passes his turn. If all players pass twice, in consecutive turns, the game ends.

Do not use a dictionary or word guide while a game is in progress to search for words to fit the tiles on your rack. The dictionary or word guide may only be consulted after a word has been played and challenged.

INTERPRETING THE RULES

Since Scrabble enjoys the two qualities that make for a truly successful game - easy to learn, but difficult to master - difficulties with interpretation of the rules are rare. As far as scoring is concerned, as long as you make sure you have fully counted every new word you have made in your turn, including all the premium word squares, you should have no problems.

Where difficulties can arise is in answering the apparently simple question: what is a word? The simple answer is to use Chambers *Official Scrabble Words*. This lists all allowable words from two to nine letters, in strict alphabetical order, including all derivatives. Thus plurals of nouns, inflexions of verbs, and comparatives and superlatives of adjective are all listed, if allowed. *The Chambers Dictionary* is the source for *Official Scrabble Words* (usually referred to as OSW, and even known affectionately by some Scrabble players as Oswald).

But what if you do not have OSW to hand? Which affixes or inflexions should you allow to the words listed in whichever dictionary you are using?

Most dictionaries show which part of speech a word is immediately after the word itself - a small n. to represent noun, v. or vb. for verb, etc.

NOUNS

If the word is a noun, you should allow it to form a plural, e.g. CHAIR – CHAIRS, WITCH – WITCHES, BERRY - BERRIES, etc. Even if a noun does not sound as if it ought to have a plural, it is a good argument-preventer to allow all plurals, unless your dictionary specifically states otherwise. Words such as MUSICS, GOLFS and GRAVIES should all be allowed. Larger dictionaries often show further meanings for words like these as well as the well-known meanings, and these further meanings will often admit a plural. For instance, one meaning of MUSIC listed in *Chambers* is `a band of musicians', which would clearly imply a plural, MUSICS.

As for irregular plurals, e.g. OX – OXEN, most dictionaries will specifically state these, and in cases of doubt, the dictionary should always be taken as the final arbiter of a plural. But where the dictionary says nothing, you can assume a regular plural exists.

VERBS

If the word is a verb, the normal -S, -ED and -ING endings can be assumed unless the dictionary states otherwise, as long as your dictionary shows irregular forms where these exist. For instance, WALK - WALKS, WALKED, WALKING or LIVE - LIVES, LIVED, LIVING. Accepted rules of spelling such as the doubling of a consonant in words like DIM - DIMMED, DIMMING should be adhered to. If your dictionary does not show irregular forms such as CHOSE and CHOSEN, or SWAM and SWUM, common sense and proper spelling must prevail. Better still, get a better dictionary, or OSW.

ADJECTIVES

Adjectives can cause difficulty. Monosyllabic adjectives should normally be allowed to take comparative and superlative forms, e.g. SHORT - SHORTER, SHORTEST. As with verbs, a good dictionary will list irregular forms, such as GOOD - BETTER, BEST. But again, there are times when common sense must prevail. FIRST is an adjective, but it would be wrong to allow FIRSTER or FIRSTEST.

With two-syllable adjectives, the best rule, to avoid arguments, is to allow comparatives and superlatives where possible. Even when the result sounds rather ugly, it is reasonable to allow such words as POLITER and POLITEST, HONESTER and HONESTEST, and LIVIDER and LIVIDEST. But once more, a line must be drawn somewhere. MAGICER and MAGICEST, for instance, are clearly not acceptable, and indeed they are not allowed by OSW.

With longer adjectives, it becomes less likely that -ER and -EST forms will be acceptable. Although OSW does allow some of these forms, you may find the easiest rule is not to allow such words, if you do not have OSW. Words like INCOMPLETER or COMFORTABLEST clearly do not ring true.

Although some adjectives, by their meanings, would not seem to allow comparatives and superlatives, you should not let this worry you.

Words such as COMPLETER, UNIQUER and DEADEST are all acceptable. As with nouns, adjectives often have subsidiary meanings, which are more amenable to adding -ER and -EST, e.g. `This is the deadest party I've ever been to'.

GENERAL

Note that some words can be more than one part of speech, and a dictionary may list a word as, say, a noun, then give one or more meanings of the word as a noun, and only then will it indicate that it can also be, say, a verb. For instance, MOUSE, as well as being the noun which we all know, can also be a verb, meaning `to catch mice'. Thus, MOUSES, MOUSED and MOUSING would all be valid words.

No other inflexions should be allowed, which are not stated in your dictionary. Prefixes such as RE- and UN-, and suffixes such as -INGS, -LY or -ER (in its `agent noun' meaning of `one who does such-and-such', e.g. PEERER, DISCARDER), should not be allowed unless specifically shown in the dictionary. Note, however, that where an -ING word is shown as a *noun*, e.g. BUILDING, the plural is allowed.

It can be a good idea to note down borderline cases as they arise, and whether or not you allowed each one to be played. If you keep this list with your set, you will build up a `house list', so that you can at least be consistent with a given word from one game to the next. But probably the best idea of all is to use OSW as the arbiter for all your games of Scrabble.

OTHER RULES

If you join a Scrabble club, or, even more so, enter a Scrabble tournament, you will find that some extra rules have been introduced. Chess clocks may be used to control the time taken by each player. The moment when your move is deemed to be played, and thus when you can no longer change your mind, is defined precisely - is it when you place your tiles on the board, when you announce your score, when you press your clock, or when you replace your tiles? In fact, if clocks are being used, the pressing of the clock is taken as the point of no return.

Various other rules have been modified or elaborated on, to eliminate all doubt. After all, if you are playing for the National Championship or even the World Championship, you have to be absolutely certain that everyone is playing to the same set of rules.

For playing at home, you will almost certainly not feel the need of any of these extra rules. However, a reasonable time limit of, say, two minutes per move may be imposed; the one certainty about the game is nobody loves a slow Scrabble player.

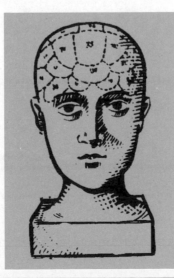

Guide Game

The Guide Game illustrates the rules and the method of scoring. It is suggested that a player set up the Guide Game on his own Scrabble board move by move according to the sequence of turns given below, counting the score for each turn and then checking it with the printed score. If he comes to a score that he does not understand, he should consult the rules to find out why the score is as it is. The Guide Game also illustrates two important characteristics of a skilfully played game

■ good distribution of words over all parts of the board
■ effective use of the premium squares with a resulting high score.

SEQUENCE OF MOVES WITH SCORES AS SHOWN IN ILLUSTRATION

PLAYER	A		PLAYER	B	
Turn	Word	Score	Turn	Word	Score
1	Horn	14	2	Farm	9
3	Paste, Farms	25	4	Mob, Not, Be	16
5	Dial, Bed	16	6	Prevent, Thorn	82
7	Models, Mobs	26	8	Quite	48
9	Prank	20	10	Six, Pranks	41
11	Hero, Me, Or, Do	27	12	Awe	12
13	Core	6	14	Zeal	26
15	Azure	15	16	Lying	39
17	Her	12	18	Tar	6
19	Conquest	212	20	Jig	22
21	Yore	21	22	To, On, An	14
23	Done, Awed	18	24	Fete, Fan, Met	18
25	Win	14	26	Lied	18
27	Give	10	28	If	5
29	Be	4	30	Cab, Ado	15
31	Up	4	32	An	2
		444			373
`A' and `I' left in hand		– 2			+ 2
Final Score		**442**	**Final Score**		**375**

Total combined score 817

	A	B	C	D	E	F	G	H	I	J	K	L	M	N	O
1	C_3			2L				3W				2L		T_1	O_1
2	O_1	2W		U_1	P_3	3L				3L			F_4	A_1	N_1
3	N_*		J_8		R_1		2L		2L			H_4	E_1	R_1	
4	Q_{10}	U_1	I_1	T_1	E_1			2L			M_3	E_1	T_1		2L
5	U_1		G_2		V_4				C_3		O_1	R_1	E_1		
6	E_1	3L			E_1	3L	I_1	F_4		A_1	D_2	O_1		W_4	
7	S_1		2L	A_1	N_1		2L	A_1	2L	B_3	E_1		2L	I_1	
8	T_1			2L	T_1	H_4	O_1	R_1	N_1		L_1	Y_4	I_1	N_1	G_2
9			2L				2L	M_3	O_1	B_3	S_1		2L		
10		3L			P_3	A_1	S_1	T_1	E_1				3L		
11				A_1	2W	R_*				D_2	I_1	A_1	L_1		
12	2L			Z_{10}	E_1	A_1	L_1	2L				W_4			L_1
13			2W	U_1		N_1	2L		G_2	I_1	V_4	E_1	2W		I_1
14		2W		R_1		K_5				3L		D_2	O_1	N_1	E_1
15	Y_4	O_1	R_1	E_1		S_1	I_1	X_8				2L			D_2

A_1 I_1

PLAYING THE GAME

The Letters

The English language version of Scrabble contains 100 letter tiles, which still follow Alfred Butts's original distribution from sixty years ago. The letters are distributed and assigned point values as follows:

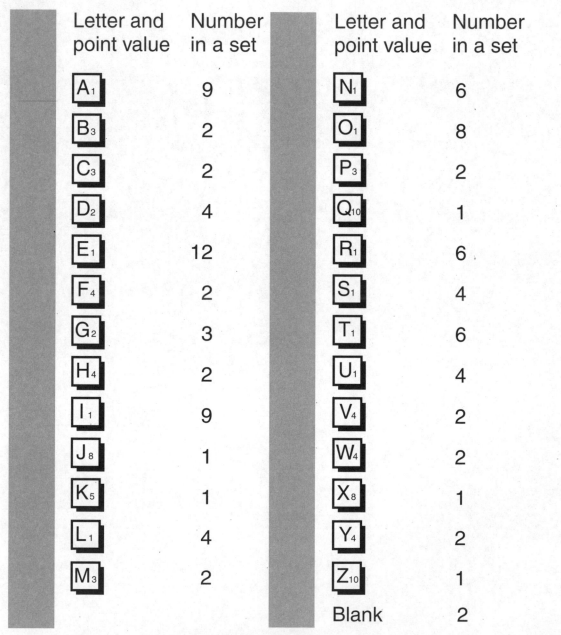

Letter and point value	Number in a set	Letter and point value	Number in a set
A_1	9	N_1	6
B_3	2	O_1	8
C_3	2	P_3	2
D_2	4	Q_{10}	1
E_1	12	R_1	6
F_4	2	S_1	4
G_2	3	T_1	6
H_4	2	U_1	4
I_1	9	V_4	2
J_8	1	W_4	2
K_5	1	X_8	1
L_1	4	Y_4	2
M_3	2	Z_{10}	1
		Blank	2

Regular Scrabble players soon learn the distribution and point value of each letter, which can help in formulating strategy and keeping check on unused tiles. It's worth noting that the division between consonants and vowels is 56 to 42, plus the two blanks.

The Board

The Scrabble board measures fifteen squares by fifteen. The squares are of five different types, coloured dark green (previously grey), light blue, dark blue, light red (pink) and dark red. The dark green squares are the `non-premium' squares, the other coloured ones are the `premium squares'. The squares are arranged on the Scrabble board like this:

Dark green squares	164	(73 per cent of the board)
Light blue squares	24	(11 per cent of the board)
Dark blue squares	12	(5 per cent of the board)
Light red (pink) squares	17	($7\frac{1}{2}$ per cent of the board)
Dark red squares	8	($3\frac{1}{2}$ per cent of the board)

The layout of the squares on a standard Scrabble board is shown below. For the purposes of this book the premium squares are marked: **2L**, **3L**, **2W** and **3W**. These correspond to the standard board as follows:

Light blue square	DOUBLE LETTER SCORE – 2L
Dark blue square	TRIPLE LETTER SCORE – 3L
Light red (pink) square	DOUBLE WORD SCORE – 2W
Dark red square	TRIPLE WORD SCORE – 3W

The starred square at the centre of the board represents the double-word-score square, which must be covered by the first word played during a game.

	A	B	C	D	E	F	G	H	I	J	K	L	M	N	O
1	3W			2L				3W				2L			3W
2		2W				3L				3L				2W	
3			2W				2L		2L				2W		
4	2L			2W				2L				2W			2L
5					2W						2W				
6		3L				3L				3L				3L	
7			2L				2L		2L				2L		
8	3W			2L				*				2L			3W
9			2L				2L		2L				2L		
10		3L				3L				3L				3L	
11					2W						2W				
12	2L			2W				2L				2W			2L
13			2W				2L		2L				2W		
14		2W				3L				3L				2W	
15	3W			2L				3W				2L			3W

Question Time

As National Scrabble Clubs Manager I am regularly asked questions about the game, the majority of which can be encompassed by the dozen broad areas of enquiry featured here. Of course I am always ready to answer questions of any sort on Scrabble and if the answer you need isn't given below, please drop me a line: at Scrabble Clubs UK, Richard House, Enstone Road, Enfield, Middlesex, EN3 7TB.

1   Can I place letters on both ends of a word in the same move? For instance BAT is on the board and I want to convert it into DEBATED.
    Yes, this is a legitimate move.

2   My opponent has played a word which ends one letter away from a double-/triple-word square. The word can be pluralized and I wish to play another word as well, how do I calculate the score? For example BAT is on the board.

I play PINS and pluralize BAT into BATS. The S falls on a double-word square but no other premium squares are involved.

The score is calculated like this:

LETTER	VALUE	SCORE
B	3	
A	1	
T	1	
S	1	
	6×2	12
P	3	
I	1	
N	1	
S	1	
	6×2	12
Total Score		24

3   I have played a word which covers two triple-word squares in one move. How much do I score?
    As outlined in rule 13, the total value of the squares is trebled and then re-trebled, so that you score nine times the value of the letters.

4   Can a blank on the board be exchanged for the letter it represents by any player?
    No, in the standard rules blanks cannot be exchanged. (Some players do play a variant of the standard rules where this is permitted).

5   What constitutes the end of a turn?

Once a player has made his move and announces his score the move is ended. Up to this point changes may still be made to the move.

6   When can I consult a dictionary?
A dictionary may only be consulted once a turn has been completed as above. It is best to use a neutral person to check the words as sometimes other useful information can be obtained accidentally whilst checking the word.

7   Which dictionary do you recommend for playing Scrabble?
Official Scrabble Words (OSW), *published by Chambers, is the officially recognized authority on allowable words in Scrabble (in the UK).*

8   Where can I obtain a two-letter word list?
All two- and three-letter words with meanings are listed at the back of OSW. A two-letter word list is included in the De Luxe version of Scrabble. (You should also find the word lists that follow later in this book useful).

9   Can the two-letter word list be used in play?
Going by the official rules no lists can be consulted during a play. However, many `friendly' games permit the use of such a list.

10   What is a good score?
An aggregate score of over 700 would be regarded as a fair score. Therefore: in a two-player game 350 is good; in a three-player game 230 is good; in a four-player game 180 is good.

11   How can I join a Scrabble Club?
Write for a list of clubs to: Scrabble Clubs (UK), Richard House, Enstone Road, Enfield, Middlesex EN3 7TB. (Scrabble clubs are covered in greater detail later in the book.)

12   Can I play Scrabble competitively?
Every year Scrabble Clubs (UK) organize the following championships:
Schools Under-16 Championship
The British Amateur Scrabble Championship – for the more socially oriented, less experienced player.
The National Scrabble Championship – for the experienced, dedicated player.
The Association of Premier Scrabble Players stage a number of tournaments around the country for all standards of player. Membership details are available from: APSP, 209 Fidlas Road, Llanishen, Cardiff CF4 5NA.
A World Scrabble Championship is held bi-annually in odd-numbered years.   ❏

S

C

R

A

B

B

L

E

What, how and why

S · C · R · A · B · B · L · E

The official rules of Scrabble state that `any words listed in a standard English dictionary are permitted, except those only spelt with an initial capital letter, abbreviations, prefixes and suffixes and words requiring apostrophes and hyphens'. Simple enough, on the face of it, but, as you may have found out in your own Scrabble games, open to all sorts of debate, differing interpretation, and dissent.

What, for instance, is an abbreviation? Is it the same as a contraction? And if the dictionary says something is `short for' something else, does that make it an abbreviation? And if a word like SNUFFBOX has got SNUFF at the end of one line, then a hyphen, then BOX at the beginning of the next line, is that a hyphen because it has always got a hyphen, or just a hyphen because the line-break happens to come in the middle of it?

When people started to form Scrabble clubs and organize tournaments in the early 1970s, there was a need for uniformity in deciding points like these. One club produced a Word Rules booklet, with thirty-odd pages of

guidance on when a word was a word, but even that could not cover every eventuality. For instance, it said that a one-syllable adjective could have a comparative and superlative (i.e. -ER and -EST endings); but the word LAND, in one of its meanings, is an adjective – as in a LAND animal. Could you, then, have LANDER and LANDEST animals? Is a dog lander than a frog? Clearly not.

Some progress has been made by them in that, in the UK, *The Chambers Dictionary* had been chosen as the standard reference book in official Scrabble circles. *Chambers* replaced the *Shorter Oxford Dictionary*, which had the distinct disadvantage of starting every entry with a capital. This change was a massive upheaval for Scrabble club members, who had to learn and unlearn thousands of words which were in *Chambers* but not *Oxford* or vice versa. For instance, in the *Oxford* days, a good player knew that the letters ACENORT made one seven-letter word, ORCANET. When the change-over took place, he or she had to forget ORCANET, which wasn't in *Chambers*, and learn the word which *Chambers* did have – ENACTOR.

The Americans meanwhile had taken a lead by publishing the *Official Scrabble Players Dictionary* (OSPD). Based on a combination of various American dictionaries, it listed all valid words from two to eight letters, with all valid derivatives given at each entry. So if an adjective had an allowed comparative and superlative, they would be listed at that adjective. This was the first comprehensive word list specifically for Scrabble, and as such was a major breakthrough.

OSPD did list meanings, but only in a very brief note form. When a word was more than one part of speech, it gave a meaning only for the part which implied the appropriate derivatives. For instance, WALK would be shown as a verb, with the endings -S, -ED and -ING. Since WALK as a noun implied only an ending of -S, which was already covered by the verb, no mention was made that WALK could be a noun at all.

This led to some rather startling entries. Anyone picking up OSPD and engaging in the usual schoolboy pursuit of looking up SEX would find that all it meant was `to ascertain the gender of' – as in sexing chickens. As this indicated the validity of SEXES, -ED and -ING, there was no need to go into the matter any further, thus helping keep everyone's mind on the Scrabble.

Then, in 1988, the big moment arrived for Scrabble players in this country – *Official Scrabble Words* (OSW) was published by Chambers. As in all aspects of life we were a few years behind the Americans, but to make up for the delay, OSW was even better than OSPD. It listed all words up to and including those with nine letters, not eight. It spelt out all valid derivatives in full in their correct alphabetical place, not under a main head-word. And in an avant garde move which stunned conventional dictionary critics, it gave no meanings at all.

Column after column, page after page, the words rolled on: DSOMOS, HICCOUGHING, PETASUSES, SENSIBLEST. At last, Scrabble players knew they would get a totally consistent, authoritative and unbiased adjudication on whether this word or that was allowed. It was like divine revelation – the Gospel according to Chambers.

Only one development is still to come in the world of Scrabble words. We use Chambers, the Americans use OSPD. Other English-speaking countries around the world use one or other or both. If a Briton wants to play serious Scrabble in America, or vice versa, the whole dreary business of learning and unlearning has to start again, then slam into reverse on the return to native shores. For the World Championship, held every two years since 1991, words in either book are allowable. It seems only a matter of time until one unified listing is produced for the whole Anglophonic world.

After all, as I said to an American player recently, `It is all one language, isn't that right, mate?'

`Ain't that the truth, buddy,' he replied.

SCRABBLE® strategy and tactics

How do tactics and strategy fit into Scrabble? Can you plan your way to victory? In part, yes. Of course, if the titles resolutely refuse to come your way, all the planning in the world will be no help. And word-power is required too; no top Scrabble player would dream of sitting down to a game without knowing all the two-letter words, all or the vast majority of the threes, plenty of useful fours and fives, and a large selection of the most likely seven- and eight-letter words which can lead to a 50-point bonus. But tactics and strategy can play a part.

First of all, what's the difference? My copy of *Fowler's Modern English Usage* (1965, price one guinea, but still, I hope, equal to the task) defines `tactics' as `the art of handling forces in battle in the immediate presence of the enemy', while `strategy' is `generalship perhaps better than any other indicates the dividing line between tactics and strategy).

So now we know. Before we even sit down, we must conceive our grand plan, our strategy. The main strategic decision a player has to make is whether to aim for an `open' or a `blocked' board. Open boards are those where there are lots of available moves, all sectors of the board are usable, and high scores are likely. Blocked boards, by contrast, offer few places to play, close off large areas of the board, and usually result in a low-scoring game.

(An open board is illustrated overleaf)

Row	1	2	3	4	5	6	7	8	9	10	11	12	13	14	15
3			2W				2L		2L				2W		
4	2L			R$_1$	2W			2L				2W			2L
5				A$_1$		2W					2W				
6		3L		V$_4$		3L				3L				3L	
7	H$_4$	E$_1$	A$_1$	T$_1$			2L		2L				2L		
8	3W			M$_3$	A$_1$	N$_1$	A$_1$	G$_2$	E$_1$			2L			3W
9			2L				2L	I$_1$	2L				2L		
10		3L				3L		V$_4$		3L				3L	
11					2W			E$_1$		G$_2$	2W				
12	2L			2W			I$_1$	N$_1$	T$_1$	A$_1$	K$_5$	E$_1$			2L
13			2W				2L		2L	Z$_{10}$			2W		
14		2W				3L				E$_1$				2W	
15	3W			2L				3W		D$_2$		2L			3W

An open board

Note that:

1. All areas of the board are available for play.
2. Most of the words are `expendable', e.g. INTAKE-S, MANAGE-D, S or R, C-HEAT or W-HEAT, and several letters go before RAVE.
3. There is further scope for bonus words, such as horizontally starting above the E of MANAGE, or finishing under the I of INTAKE.
4. Some of the tws squares are open for use.
5. There are several open letters for eight-letter bonus words.
6. Difficult letters such as V and Z have been placed in the middle of words, not at the beginning or end where they may prevent expansion. On the other hand, how about this board on the following page?

Here we have the quintessential blocked board. We can see that:

1. Large parts of the board are no-go areas, almost impossible to move into.
2. Few words are expandable.
3. There is little scope for bonus words.
4. Only two tws squares are immediately usable, and even on those it is difficult to achieve a high score.

Note particularly the `stepladder' leading up to the top right-hand corner, which makes it almost impossible to use the rest of the top half of the board.

A blocked board

Open or blocked?

When should you aim for an open board, and when for a blocked one? In general, try to keep the board open (a) if you think your word power is stronger than that of your opponent, (b) if you want to score a high number of points, even if your opponent may do so as well, and (c) if you have fallen behind, and need some openings for a chance to get back in the game.

Obviously, when the opposite conditions exist, you should be trying for a blocked board: (a) if you think your opponent has a stronger vocabulary than you, and (b) if the winning of the game is more important than a very high score, particularly if you are ahead by at least about 50 points.

One example should show you how to open or block a board:

Your rack is ADEEIRV.

Let us look at some of your possible moves, and their likely effect on the board.

You play VIED/FREED. This is probably the best blocking move. The `squaring off' of the corner with D makes VIED and FREED hard to expand. The V prevents a bonus from being played horizontally underneath VIED, and also blocks horizontal words in the row above finishing under the B or A. Even here, a danger lurks. IVIED is a word (covered in ivy), but a high score from it is unlikely. Even if your opponent is lucky enough to have a seven-letter word with I as the second letter, enabling him to slot in a bonus using IVIED, he will open two tws squares which you may be able to use.

You play DIV/FREED. This is a more open move. Although taking out the possibility of a bonus using FREED, FREER, FREES, or indeed FREET, it opens what is probably a better place, with the chance of making DIVA, DIVE, DIVI or DIVS. Equally, playing DIVE rather than DIV would make bonus chances with DIVED, DIVER or DIVES. If you went the whole hog and played neither DIV nor DIVE but DIVER, you are opening the chance of a bonus on the tws with DIVERS – potentially a very high score.

There are also chances for eight-letter words through the V, E or R. All of these are open moves.

You play IRE/EF. This is perhaps the most open move. You leave the bonus chances under FREE, and open a raft of new ones with all the letters that can go before IRE. There are now also chances for eight-letter words through the I or ending in R, or a high-scoring four-letter word on the tws in the top centre, such as HOAX.

A whole book could probably be written about open and blocked boards alone, but the above should be enough to give you an idea of the uses of each and how to form them.

Tile turnover

Some strategies are almost always worth playing. Top players are all familiar with the term `tile turnover'. This simply means that the more tiles you can play in each turn, the better. Imagine you are playing the opening move of the game, and your rack is ABDINRT.

You may consider playing BID, BIT or BAD, but by playing more tiles, you give yourself a better chance of improving your rack. You are more likely to pick in a blank, S or high-scorer. There are no letters which are always bad, but some which are always, or very nearly always, good, so you should maximize your chances of getting them.

You could play a four-letter word, such as BIRD or BARD; or five, like BRAND, BRAIN or TRAIN. Don't worry, incidentally, about playing your A and I. With five new tiles to pick in, you will probably get a couple of vowels. Playing five letters also allows you to use a dls square.

Can you play six letters? Trickier, but with some judicious shuffling you should see BANDIT or RIBAND. BANDIT scores 24 with the B on the dls square, and does not give many chances to your opponent. Much better than BID; a higher score, fewer openings for your opponent to use, and three more chances to get those lovely Ss and blanks.

Of course the best move, if you know it and spot it, would be to maximize your tile turnover by playing ANTBIRD for 74. But even expert players could well miss that one. At this stage, be reasonably satisfied if you found BANDIT or RIBAND.

So there are a couple of strategies for you to think about. Now, how about those tactics?

	A	B	C	D	E	F	G	H	I	J	K	L	M	N	O
1	3W			2L			E_1	R_1				2L			3W
2		2W				3L	O_1	H_4		3L			2W		
3			2W				N_1	O_1	M_3				2W		
4	2L			2W				2L	U_1		B_3	A_1	N_1		2L
5					2W		Z_{10}	A_1	N_1	I_1	E_1	R_1			
6		3L				3L			T_1	3L			3L		
7			2L				2L		I_1			2L			
8	3W			2L		C_3	R_1	A_1	N_1			2L			3W
9			2L				2L		G_2			2L			
10		3L				H_4	I_1	P_3	S_1	3L			3L		
11					2W						2W				

Rack Management

This is another term you will hear bandied about when top players gather to relive old glories or curse their bad luck. Take a situation like that above:

Your rack is AAEIPTW.

There are several possibilities. You could jump in with WEPT/WHIPS. That scores 31, but look at what you have left on your rack AAI. If you pick another couple of vowels, you could end up with a vowel-heavy selection with which you can do very little. So what about WIPE in the same place? Better, but you still have an awkward double A. You could pick one more and have three As next turn – a real handicap.

Ideally, you want to play at least two vowels, one of which is an A. If you aim to keep anything, keep the E, although even that is not a priority – with just two Es on the board, you should get another one soon enough.

WAIN, using the N of BAN, would fit the bill, but scores only 14. AWA and HA, using the H of HIPS, scores 17, but perhaps the best, bearing in mind your tile turnover strategy, is AWAIT, making HI and IT. That scores 23, balances the rack, and turns over five tiles, although it does provide possible bonus places for your opponent, such as a seven-letter word starting with S which turns IT into ITS.

Of course, he could make his bonus anyway by turning BAN into BANS, but that would open a tws for you. Meanwhile, you have managed your rack well, and given yourself five chances to pick an S or a blank, so, all in all, you can be well satisfied with your move.

Shepherding

Another very useful tactic is that of, to coin a phrase for it, shepherding, in which you make your opponent go where you want, not where he wants. Look at this board.

	1	2	3	4	5	6	7	8	9	10	11	12	13	14	15
1	3W			2L				3W				2L			3W
2		2W				3L				3L				2W	
3			2W				2L		2L				2W		
4	2L			2W				O_1				2W			2L
5					2W			E_1	H_4		2W				
6		3L				3L			I_1	3L				3L	
7			G_2	N_1	U_1		2L		L_1				2L		
8	3W		L_1	2L	G_2	N_1	A_1	R_1	L_1			2L			3W
9			I_1				2L		Y_4				2L		
10		3L	B_3	O_1	X_8	3L				3L				3L	
11					2W						2W				
12	2L			2W				2L				2W			2L

Your rack is AEILOST. Great! You've spotted that elusive bonus. Haven't you? ISOLATE. Now, where to play it. ISOLATE/XI scores 73, while ISOLATE/TOE scores 70, so go for XI, right? Wrong.

Place ISOLATE/XI on the board, and you will see you have opened a great chance for your opponent. If he has a D or S, he can make ISOLATED or ISOLATES, doubling whatever word he makes and adding 16 for ISOLATES or 18 for ISOLATED. If he has a seven-letter word ending in D or S, he quadruples his score for it. Unless your strategy is to play ultra-open, this is much too dangerous.

Now look at ISOLATE/TOE. You have blocked off a dangerous opening, with so many letters able to precede -OE. And by playing in the *third* row, you force your opponent, if he has a bonus, to play in the *second* row if he cannot fit it into one of the more difficult openings elsewhere, which gives you a chance to go to town on the tws squares on the top row. You have maximized the chance of your opponent going where you want him to. Scrabble meets One Man and His Dog.

So there you are. Opening and blocking the board, tile turnover, rack management and shepherding; just some of the strategies and tactics you can now start practising to improve and develop your play. ❑

WORD LISTS

There's more to building a vocabulary for playing Scrabble than simply trying to learn words at random. In the next section you can read how leading players set about extending and improving their vocabularies. For players at all levels *Official Scrabble Lists* (OSL) published by Chambers is an indispensable aid and I am very grateful to Chambers Harrap Publishers Ltd for their permission to include the following lists, or extracts from lists, taken from the 1995 edition of OSL.

Official Scrabble Lists is based on *Official Scrabble Words*, the official UK authority for allowable Scrabble words, and the latest edition of OSL has been compiled by Allan Simmons and Darryl Francis, two leading Scrabble players of whom you will read more later in this book. If you want to check on the meanings of any of the words listed, they can all be found in *The Chambers Dictionary*.

Two-letter words

The correct use of two-letter words lies at the heart of successful Scrabble playing. Two-letter words make it possible to play words parallel to other words on the board. A lot of them can have letters added to make valid longer words in later moves. There are 109 allowable two-letter words. All are listed here and every player wanting to improve his or her play will try to learn all of them.

2-LETTER WORDS				
AA	BO	GO	MA	OO	TI
AD	BY	GU	ME	OR	TO
AE	CH	HA	MI	OS	UG
AH	DA	HE	MO	OU	UM
AI	DI	HI	MU	OW	UN
AM	DO	HO	MY	OX	UP
AN	EA	ID	NA	OY	UR
AR	EE	IF	NE	PA	US
AS	EF	IN	NO	PH	UT
AT	EH	IO	NU	PI	WE
AW	EL	IS	NY	PO	WO
AX	EM	IT	OB	QI	XI
AY	EN	JO	OD	RE	XU
BA	ER	KA	OE	SH	YE
BE	ES	KO	OF	SI	YO
BI	EX	KY	OH	SO	YU
	FA	LA	OI	ST	ZO
	FY	LI	OM	TA	
	GI	LO	ON	TE	

Three-letter words

Learning more than 1100 three-letter words may seem a tall order, but many of them will be familiar already. Three-letter words are useful for converting two-letter words into potentially high-scoring words and generally for making useful scoring moves on otherwise unpromising boards. Once again all the ones in OSL are given.

3–LETTER WORDS			
AAS	AGO	ALS	ARK
ABA	AHA	ALT	ARM
ABB	AHS	AMI	ARS
ABY	AIA	AMP	ART
ACE	AID	ANA	ARY
ACH	AIL	AND	ASH
ACT	AIM	ANE	ASK
ADD	AIN	ANI	ASP
ADO	AIR	ANN	ASS
ADS	AIS	ANT	ATE
ADZ	AIT	ANY	AUF
AFT	AKE	APE	AUK
AGA	ALA	APT	AVA
AGE	ALB	ARB	AVE
	ALE	ARC	AWA
	ALL	ARD	AWE
	ALP	ARE	AWL

AWN	BOR	COZ	DOR
AXE	BOS	CRU	DOS
AYE	BOT	CRY	DOT
AYS	BOW	CUB	DOW
AYU	BOX	CUD	DRY
BAA	BOY	CUE	DSO
BAD	BRA	CUM	DUB
BAG	BRO	CUP	DUD
BAH	BUB	CUR	DUE
BAM	BUD	CUT	DUG
BAN	BUG	CUZ	DUN
BAP	BUM	CWM	DUO
BAR	BUN	DAB	DUP
BAS	BUR	DAD	DUX
BAT	BUS	DAE	DYE
BAY	BUT	DAG	DZO
BED	BUY	DAH	EAN
BEE	BYE	DAK	EAR
BEG	BYS	DAL	EAS
BEL	CAB	DAM	EAT
BEN	CAD	DAN	EAU
BET	CAM	DAP	EBB
BEY	CAN	DAS	ECH
BEZ	CAP	DAW	ECO
BIB	CAR	DAY	ECU
BID	CAT	DEB	EDH
BIG	CAW	DEE	EEK
BIN	CAY	DEF	EEL
BIO	CEE	DEI	EEN
BIS	CEL	DEL	EFF
BIT	CEP	DEN	EFS
BIZ	CHA	DEW	EFT
BOA	CHE	DEY	EGG
BOB	CHI	DIB	EGO
BOD	CID	DID	EHS
BOG	CIG	DIE	EIK
BOH	CIT	DIG	EKE
BOK	CLY	DIM	ELD
BON	COB	DIN	ELF
BOO	COD	DIP	ELK
BOP	COG	DIT	ELL
	COL	DIV	ELM
	CON	DOB	ELS
	COO	DOC	ELT
	COP	DOD	EME
	COR	DOE	EMS
	COS	DOG	EMU
	COT	DOH	END
	COW	DON	ENE
	COX	DOO	ENG
	COY	DOP	ENS

EON	FIE	GIB	HET
ERA	FIG	GID	HEW
ERE	FIL	GIE	HEX
ERF	FIN	GIF	HEY
ERG	FIR	GIG	HIC
ERK	FIT	GIN	HID
ERN	FIX	GIO	HIE
ERR	FIZ	GIP	HIM
ERS	FLU	GIS	HIN
ESS	FLY	GIT	HIP
EST	FOB	GJU	HIS
ETA	FOE	GNU	HIT
ETH	FOG	GOA	HOA
EUK	FOH	GOB	HOB
EVE	FON	GOD	HOC
EWE	FOP	GOE	HOD
EWK	FOR	GON	HOE
EWT	FOU	GOO	HOG
EYE	FOX	GOS	HOH
FAB	FOY	GOT	HOI
FAD	FRA	GOV	HON
FAG	FRO	GOY	HOO
FAH	FRY	GUB	HOP
	FUB	GUE	HOS
	FUD	GUM	HOT
	FUG	GUN	HOW
	FUM	GUP	HOX
	FUN	GUR	HOY
	FUR	GUS	HUB
	GAB	GUT	HUE
	GAD	GUV	HUG
	GAE	GUY	HUH
	GAG	GYM	HUI
FAN	GAL	GYP	HUM
FAP	GAM	HAD	HUP
FAR	GAN	HAE	HUT
FAS	GAP	HAG	HYE
FAT	GAR	HAH	HYP
FAW	GAS	HAJ	ICE
FAX	GAT	HAM	ICH
FAY	GAU	HAN	ICY
FED	GAY	HAP	IDE
FEE	GED	HAS	IDS
FEN	GEE	HAT	IFF
FET	GEL	HAW	IFS
FEU	GEM	HAY	ILK
FEW	GEN	HEM	ILL
FEY	GEO	HEN	IMP
FEZ	GET	HEP	INK
FIB	GEY	HER	INN
FID	GHI	HES	INS

ION	KAT	LEV	MES
IOS	KAW	LEW	MET
IRE	KAY	LEX	MEU
IRK	KEA	LEY	MEW
ISH	KEB	LEZ	MHO
ISM	KED	LIB	MID
ISO	KEF	LID	MIL
ITA	KEG	LIE	MIM
ITS	KEN	LIG	MIR
IVY	KEP	LIN	MIS
JAB	KET	LIP	MIX
JAG	KEX	LIS	MIZ
JAK	KEY	LIT	MNA
JAM	KID	LOB	MOA
JAP	KIF	LOG	MOB
JAR	KIN	LOO	MOD
JAW	KIP	LOP	MOE
JAY	KIR	LOR	MOG
JEE	KIT	LOS	MOI
JET	KOA	LOT	MOM
JEU	KOB	LOW	MON
JEW	KON	LOX	MOO
JIB	KOP	LOY	MOP
JIG	KOS	LUD	MOR
JIZ	KOW	LUG	MOT
JOB	KYE	LUM	MOU
JOE	KYU	LUR	MOW
JOG	LAB	LUV	MOY
JOR	LAC	LUX	MOZ
	LAD	LUZ	MUD
	LAG	LYE	MUG
	LAH	LYM	MUM
	LAM	MAA	MUN
	LAP	MAC	MUS
	LAR	MAD	MUX
	LAS	MAE	NAB
	LAT	MAG	NAE
	LAV	MAK	NAG
	LAW	MAL	NAM
	LAX	MAM	NAN
JOT	LAY	MAN	NAP
JOW	LEA	MAP	NAS
JOY	LED	MAR	NAT
JUD	LEE	MAS	NAY
JUG	LEG	MAT	NEB
JUS	LEI	MAW	NED
JUT	LEK	MAX	NEE
KAE	LEP	MAY	NEF
KAI	LES	MEG	NEK
KAM	LET	MEL	NEP
KAS	LEU	MEN	NET

36

NEW	OKE	PEN	QUA
NIB	OLD	PEP	RAD
NID	OLE	PER	RAG
NIE	OLM	PET	RAH
NIL	OMS	PEW	RAI
NIM	ONE	PHI	RAJ
NIP	ONS	PHO	RAM
NIS	OOF	PHS	RAN
NIT	OOH	PIA	RAP
NIX	OOM	PIC	RAS
NOB	OON	PIE	RAT
NOD	OOP	PIG	
NOG	OOR	PIN	
NOH	OOS	PIP	
NOM	OPE	PIR	
NON	OPT	PIS	
NOR	ORB	PIT	
NOS	ORC	PIU	
NOT	ORD	PIX	
NOW	ORE	PLY	
NOX	ORF	POA	
NOY	ORS	POD	
NTH	ORT	POH	RAW
NUB	OUK	POI	RAX
NUN	OUP	POM	RAY
NUR	OUR	POO	REC
NUS	OUT	POP	RED
NUT	OVA	POS	REE
NYE	OWE	POT	REF
NYS	OWL	POW	REH
OAF	OWN	POX	REM
OAK	OWT	POZ	REN
OAR	OYE	PRE	REP
OAT	OYS	PRO	RES
OBA	PAD	PRY	RET
OBI	PAH	PSI	REV
OBO	PAL	PST	REW
OBS	PAM	PUB	REX
OCA	PAN	PUD	REZ
OCH	PAP	PUG	RHO
ODA	PAR	PUH	RHY
ODD	PAS	PUN	RIA
ODE	PAT	PUP	RIB
ODS	PAW	PUR	RID
OES	PAX	PUS	RIG
OFF	PAY	PUT	RIM
OFT	PEA	PUY	RIN
OHM	PEC	PYE	RIP
OHO	PED	PYX	RIT
OIK	PEE	QAT	RIZ
OIL	PEG	QIS	ROB
			ROC

37

ROD	SIN	TAN	TWO
ROE	SIP	TAP	TWP
ROK	SIR	TAR	TYE
ROM	SIS	TAT	TYG
ROO	SIT	TAU	UDO
ROT	SIX	TAW	UDS
ROW	SKA	TAX	UEY
RUB	SKI	TAY	UFO
RUC	SKY	TEA	UGH
RUD	SLY	TED	UGS
RUE	SMA	TEE	UKE
RUG	SNY	TEF	ULE
RUM	SOB	TEG	UNI
RUN	SOC	TEL	UNS
RUT	SOD	TEN	UPS
RYA	SOG	TES	URD
RYE	SOH	TEW	URE
SAB	SOL	THE	URN
SAC	SON	THO	USE
SAD	SOP	THY	UTE
SAE	SOS	TIC	UTS
SAG	SOT	TID	UTU
SAI	SOU	TIE	UVA
SAL	SOV	TIG	VAC
SAM	SOW	TIL	VAE
SAN	SOX	TIN	VAN
SAP	SOY	TIP	VAS
SAR	SPA	TIS	
SAT	SPY	TIT	
SAW	STY	TOC	
SAX	SUB	TOD	
SAY	SUD	TOE	
SAZ	SUE	TOG	
SEA	SUI	TOM	
SEC	SUK	TON	
SED	SUM	TOO	
SEE	SUN	TOP	
SEG	SUP	TOR	
SEI	SUQ	TOT	
SEL	SUR	TOW	VAT
SEN	SUS	TOY	VAU
SET	SWY	TRY	VEE
SEW	SYE	TUB	VEG
SEX	TAB	TUG	VET
SEY	TAD	TUI	VEX
SEZ	TAE	TUM	VIA
SHE	TAG	TUN	VID
SHY	TAI	TUP	VIE
SIB	TAJ	TUT	VIM
SIC	TAK	TUX	VIN
SIM	TAM	TWA	VIS
			VLY

38

VOE	YAM
VOL	YAP
VOR	YAW
VOW	YEA
VOX	YEN
VUG	YEP
VUM	YES
WAD	YET
WAE	YEW
WAG	YEX
WAN	YGO
WAP	YIN
WAR	YIP
WAS	YOB
WAT	YOD
WAW	YOK
WAX	YON
WAY	YOS
WEB	YOU
WED	YOW
WEE	YUG
WEM	YUK
WEN	YUP
WET	YUS
WEX	ZAG
WEY	ZAP
WHA	ZAX
WHO	ZEA
WHY	ZED
WIG	ZEE
WIN	ZEK
WIS	ZEL
WIT	ZEX
WOE	ZHO
WOG	ZIG
WOK	ZIP
WON	ZIT
WOO	ZIZ
WOP	ZOA
WOS	ZOO
WOT	ZOS
WOW	ZUZ
WOX	
WRY	
WUD	
WUS	
WYE	
WYN	
XIS	
YAH	
YAK	

LIGHT WORDS (Many vowels)

Light words, words with a lot of vowels, are useful for discarding surplus vowels in the hope that you can achieve a better balanced rack. This is the list for two- to five-letter words. Inflections ending in -S have been omitted.

2–letter words – 2 vowels
AA AE AI EA EE IO OE OI OO OU

3–LETTER WORDS – 3 VOWELS
AIA EAU
AII
AIO

4–letter words – 3 vowels or more (by vowel content)

			BEAU
			EAUS
			EAUX
			UREA
			UVAE
			UVEA
		AII	ILIA
			INIA
			IXIA
		AIO	AGIO
			CIAO
			IOTA
AAE	ALAE		IAO
	AREA		NAOI
AAI	AIAS		OBIA
	ARIA	AIU	AITU
AAO	ANOA		HUIA
AAU	AQUA	AOU	AUTO
	AULA		URAO
	AURA	AUU	LUAU
	PAUA		UNAU
AEE	AGEE	EEE	EPEE
	AJEE	EEI	EINE
	AKEE		IDEE
	ALEE	EEO	EVOE
	EALE		OGEE
	EASE	EEU	EMEU
AEI	AIDE		EUGE
	AINE	EIOU	EUOI
	AMIE	EIU	ETUI
	IDEA		IURE
	ILEA		LIEU
	KAIE	EOO	OBOE
	VIAE		OLEO
AEO	AEON		OOSE
	AERO		OOZE
	ALOE	EOU	EURO
	EOAN		MOUE
	ODEA		ROUE
	TOEA	IOO	MOOI
	ZOEA		OLIO
AEU	AGUE	OOU	UOZO
	AUNE		

5–letter words – 4 vowels or more (by vowel content)			AEEI	AERIE AINEE	AEOO AIIO	ZOOEA AIDOI	EEEI	OUIJA EERIE
			AEEO	ZOEAE		AIOLI	EEOO	COOEE
			AEIU	ADIEU		OIDIA	EEUU	QUEUE
AAEI	AECIA			AUREI	AIOU	AUDIO	EIOO	OORIE
AAEU	AQUAE			URAEI		AULOI	EIOU	OURIE
	AURAE							

HEAVY WORDS (Many Consonants) except -S inflections

As the name suggests, heavy words are the opposite of light words, having a preponderance of consonants. Their use lies in providing a means of disposing of surplus consonants in order to try to get a better balanced rack. This is the list for two- to five-letter words. Inflections ending in -S have been omitted.

2–letter words – no vowels except Y
BY CH FY KY MY NY PH SH ST

3–letter words – no vowels except Y
CLY
CRY
CWM
DRY
FLY
FRY
GYM
GYP
HYP
LYM
NTH
NYS
PLY
PRY
PST
PYX
RHY
SHY
SKY
SLY
SNY
SPY
STY
SWY
THY
TRY
TWP
TYG
VLY
WHY
WRY
WYN

4–letter words – no vowels except Y
BRRR
CYST
FYRD
GYMP
GYNY
HWYL
HYMN
JYNX
KYND
LYNX
MYTH
PRYS
PSST
RYND
SCRY
SKRY
SKYR

SPRY
SYNC
SYND
TRYP
TYMP
TYND
WYCH
WYND
WYNN
XYST
YMPT

5–letter words – no vowels except Y
CHYND
CRWTH
CRYPT
DRYLY
GHYLL
GLYPH
GRYPT
GYNNY
GYPPY
GYPSY
KYDST
LYMPH
LYNCH
MYRRH
NYMPH
PSYCH
PYGHY
SHYLY
SLYLY
SYLPH
SYNCH
SYNTH
THYMY
TRYST
WRYLY
XYLYL

High Scorers

There are four high-scoring letters in Scrabble: J, Q, X and Z. Most Scrabble players know at least a few words containing them, but in each case the list of allowable words is much greater than might at first be imagined.
Official Scrabble Lists contains all the allowable words from two- to eight-letters long for each of the high-scoring letters. Here, to give an idea of the range of words available to players prepared to learn them, we list the words from two- to five-letters long for J, Q, X and Z.

J-WORDS

J – 2–letter words
JO

J – 3–letter words
GJU
HAJ
JAB
JAG
JAK
JAM
JAP
JAR
JAW
JAY

JEE	JATO	JOOK	EJECT
JET	JAUP	JORS	ENJOY
JEU	JAWS	JOSH	FALAJ
JEW	JAYS	JOSS	FJORD
JIB	JAZY	JOTA	GADJE
JIG	JAZZ	JOTS	GAJOS
JIZ	JEAN	JOUK	GANJA
JOB	JEAT	JOUR	GAUJE
JOE	JEED	JOWL	HADJI
JOG	JEEL	JOWS	HAJES
JOR	JEER	JOYS	HAJIS
JOT	JEES	JUBA	HAJJI
JOW	JEFF	JUBE	HEJAB
JOY	JELL	JUDO	HEJRA
JUD	JERK	JUDS	HIJAB
JUG	JESS	JUDY	HIJRA
JUS	JEST	JUGA	HODJA
JUT	JETE	JUGS	JABOT
RAJ	JETS	JUJU	JACKS
TAJ	JEUX	JUKE	JADED
	JEWS	JUMP	JADES
	JIAO	JUNK	JAGER
J – 4–letter words	JIBE	JURA	JAGGY
AJAR	JIBS	JURE	JAGIR
AJEE	JIFF	JURY	JAILS
BAJU	JIGS	JUST	JAKES
BENJ	JILL	JUTE	JALAP
DOJO	JILT	JUTS	JAMBE
GAJO	JIMP	JUVE	JAMBO
GJUS	JINK	JYNX	JAMBS
HADJ	JINN	MOJO	JAMBU
HAJI	JINX	PUJA	JAMES
HAJJ	JIRD	RAJA	JAMMY
JABS	JISM	ROJI	JANES
JACK	JIVE	SIJO	JANNS
JADE	JIZZ	SOJA	JANTY
JAGS	JOBE		JAPAN
JAIL	JOBS	**J – 5–letter words**	JAPED
JAKE	JOCK	AFLAJ	JAPER
JAKS	JOCO	AJWAN	JAPES
JAMB	JOES	BAJAN	JARKS
JAMS	JOEY	BAJRA	JARLS
JANE	JOGS	BAJRI	JARTA
JANN	JOHN	BAJUS	JARUL
JAPE	JOIN	BANJO	JASEY
JAPS	JOKE	BIJOU	JASPE
JARK	JOKY	BUNJE	JASPS
JARL	JOLE	BUNJY	JATOS
JARS	JOLL	CAJUN	JAUNT
JASP	JOLT	DJINN	JAUPS
JASS	JOMO	DOJOS	JAVEL
JASY			

S
C
R
A
B
B
L
E

JAWAN	JIVES	JUKED	SAJOU
JAWED	JNANA	JUKES	SHOJI
JAZZY	JOBED	JULEP	SIJOS
JEANS	JOBES	JUMAR	SOJAS
JEATS	JOCKO	JUMBO	SUJEE
JEBEL	JOCKS	JUMBY	TAJES
JEELS	JODEL	JUMPS	THUJA
JEELY	JOEYS	JUMPY	UPJET
JEERS	JOHNS	JUNCO	WILJA
JEFFS	JOINS	JUNKS	YOHAN
JEHAD	JOINT	JUNKY	ZANJA
JELAB	JOIST	JUNTA	
JELLO	JOKED	JUNTO	

Q-WORDS

Q – 2–letter words
QI

Q – 3–letter words
QAT
QIS
QUA
SUQ

Q – 4–letter words
AQUA
QADI
QATS
QOPH
QUAD
QUAG
QUAT
QUAY
QUEP
QUEY
QUID
QUIM
QUIN
QUIP
QUIT
QUIZ
QUOD
QUOP
SUQS
WAQF

Q – 5–letter words
AQUAE
AQUAS
BURQA
EQUAL
EQUID
EQUIP

JELLS	JOKER	JURAL
JELLY	JOKES	JURAT
JEMMY	JOKEY	JUROR
JENNY	JOKOL	JUSTS
JERID	JOLED	JUTES
JERKS	JOLES	JUTTY
JERKY	JOLLS	JUVES
JERRY	JOLLY	KANJI
JESTS	JOLTS	KHOJA
JESUS	JOLTY	KOPJE
JETES	JOMOS	LAPJE
JETON	JONTY	MAJOR
JETTY	JOOKS	MOJOS
JEUNE	JORAM	MUJIK
JEWED	JORUM	NINJA
JEWEL	JOTAS	
JHALA	JOTUN	
JIAOS	JOUAL	
JIBED	JOUGS	
JIBER	JOUKS	
JIBES	JOULE	
JIFFS	JOURS	
JIFFY	JOUST	
JIGOT	JOWAR	
JIHAD	JOWED	
JILLS	JOWLS	
JILTS	JOWLY	
JIMMY	JOYED	
JIMPY	JUBAS	OBJET
JINGO	JUBES	OJIME
JINKS	JUDAS	OUIJA
JINNI	JUDGE	POOJA
JINNS	JUDOS	PUJAS
JIRDS	JUGAL	RAJAH
JIRGA	JUGUM	RAJAS
JISMS	JUICE	RAJES
JIVED	JUICY	REJIG
JIVER	JUJUS	REJON
		ROJIS

MAQUI	QUIPU	HEX	EXIT
PIQUE	QUIRE	LOX	EXON
QADIS	QUIRK	LUX	EXPO
QANAT	QUIRT	MAX	EXUL
QIBLA	QUIST	MIX	FAIX
QOPHS	QUITE	MUX	FALX
QUACK	QUITS	NIX	FAUX
QUADS	QUOAD	NOX	FLAX
QUAFF	QUODS	PAX	FLEX
QUAGS	QUOIF	PIX	FLIX
QUAIL	QUOIN	POX	FLUX
QUAIR	QUOIT	PYX	FOXY
QUAKE	QUOLL	RAX	HOAX
QUAKY	QUONK	REX	IBEX
QUALE	QUOPS	SAX	ILEX
QUALM	QUOTA	SEX	IXIA
QUANT	QUOTE	SIX	JEUX
QUARE	QUOTH	SOX	JINX
QUARK	QUYTE	TAX	JYNX
QUART	ROQUE	TUX	LANX
QUASI I	SQUAB	VEX	LUXE
QUASI	SQUAD	VOX	LYNX
QUATS	SQUAT	WAX	MAXI
QUAYD	SQUAW	WEX	MINX
QUAYS	SQUEG	WOX	MIXT
QUEAN	SQUIB	XIS	MIXY
QUEEN	SQUID	YEX	MOXA
QUEER	SQUIT	ZAX	NEXT
QUELL	SQUIZ	ZEX	NIXY
QUEME	TALAQ		ONYX
QUENA	TOQUE	X – 4–letter words	ORYX
QUERN	TUQUE	APEX	OXEN
QUERY	WAQFS	AXED	OXER
QUEST		AXEL	PIXY
QUEUE		AXES	POXY
QUEYN	**X-WORDS**	AXIL	PREX
QUEYS	X – 2–letter words	AXIS	ROUX
QUICH	AX	AXLE	SEXT
QUICK	EX	AXON	SEXY
QUIDS	OX	BOXY	TAXA
QUIET	XI	CALX	TAXI
QUIFF	XU	COAX	TEXT
QUILL		COXA	ULEX
QUILT	X – 3–letter words	COXY	VEXT
QUIMS	AXE	CRUX	WAXY
QUINA	BOX	DIXI	WEXE
QUINE	COX	DIXY	XYST
QUINS	DUX	DOXY	YUNX
QUINT	FAX	EAUX	
QUIPO	FIX	EXAM	X – 5–letter words
QUIPS	FOX	EXES	ADDAX

43

ADMIX	COXED	EXULT	NOXAL
AFFIX	COXES	EXURB	NOXES
ANNEX	CULEX	FAXED	OXERS
ATAXY	CYLIX	FAXES	OXIDE
AUXIN	DESEX	FIXED	OXIME
AXELS	DETOX	FIXER	OXLIP
AXIAL	DIXIE	FIXES	OXTER
AXILE	DRUXY	FLAXY	PANAX
AXILS	DUXES	FOXED	PAXES
AXING	EMBOX	FOXES	PHLOX
AXIOM	ENFIX	HELIX	PIXEL
AXLES	EPOXY	HEXAD	PIXES
AXMAN	EXACT	HEXED	PIXIE
AXMEN	EXALT	HEXES	PODEX
AXOID	EXAMS	HOXED	POXED
AXONS	EXCEL	HOXES	POXES
		HYRAX	PREXY
		IMMIX	PROXY
		INDEX	PYXED
		INFIX	PYXES
		IXIAS	PYXIS
		IXTLE	RADIX
		KEXES	RAXED
		KYLIX	RAXES
		LATEX	REDOX
		LAXER	RELAX
		LAXES	REMEX
		LAXLY	REMIX
		LEXES	SALIX
		LEXIS	SAXES
		LIMAX	SEXED
		LOXES	SEXER
		LUXES	SEXES
BEAUX	EXEAT	MALAX	SEXTS
BOLIX	EXEEM	MAXES	SILEX
BORAX	EXEME	MAXIM	SIXER
BOXED	EXERT	MAXIS	SIXES
BOXEN	EXIES	MIXED	SIXTE
BOXER	EXILE	MIXEN	SIXTH
BOXES	EXINE	MIXER	SIXTY
BRAXY	EXIST	MIXES	SOREX
BUXOM	EXITS	MOXAS	TAXED
CALIX	EXODE	MOXIE	TAXER
CALYX	EXONS	MUREX	TAXES
CAREX	EXPAT	MUXED	TAXIS
CAXON	EXPEL	MUXES	TAXOL
CHOUX	EXPOS	NEXTS	TAXON
CIMEX	EXTOL	NEXUS	TAXOR
CODEX	EXTRA	NIXED	TELEX
COXAE	EXUDE	NIXES	TEXAS
COXAL	EXULS	NIXIE	TEXTS

44

TOXIC	JIZ	GAZE	ZEAL
TOXIN	LEZ	GAZY	ZEAS
TUXES	LUZ	GIZZ	ZEBU
UNBOX	MIZ	HAZE	ZEDS
UNFIX	MOZ	HAZY	ZEES
UNSEX	POZ	HIZZ	ZEIN
UNTAX	REZ	JAZY	ZEKS
VARIX	RIZ	JAZZ	ZELS
VEXED	SAZ	JIZZ	ZERO
VEXER	SEZ	KAZI	ZEST
VEXES	ZAG	LAZE	ZETA
VIBEX	ZAP	LAZO	ZEZE
VITEX	ZAX	LAZY	ZHOS
VIXEN	ZEA	LEZZ	ZIFF
WAXED	ZED	LUTZ	ZIGS
WAXEN	ZEE	MAZE	ZILA
WAXER	ZEK	MAZY	ZIMB
WAXES	ZEL	MEZE	ZINC
WEXED	ZEX	MIZZ	ZING
WEXES	ZHO	MOZE	ZIPS
WOXEN	ZIG	MOZZ	ZITE
XEBEC	ZIP	MZEE	ZITI
XENIA	ZIT	NAZE	ZITS
XENON	ZIZ	OOZE	ZIZZ
XERIC	ZOA	OOZY	ZOBO
XOANA	ZOD	OUZO	ZOBU
XYLEM	ZOS	OYEZ	ZOEA
XYLIC	ZUZ	PHIZ	ZOIC
XYLOL		PIZE	ZONA
XYLYL	**Z – 4–letter words**	POZZ	ZONE
XYSTI	ADZE	PUTZ	ZONK
XYSTS	AZAN	QUIZ	ZOOM
YEXED	AZYM	RAZE	ZOON
YEXES	BOZO	RAZZ	ZOOS
ZAXES	BUZZ	RIZA	ZOPP
ZEXES	CHEZ	SIZE	ZOUK
	CHIZ	SIZY	ZULU
	COZE	SWIZ	ZUPA
	COZY	TIZZ	ZURF
Z-WORDS	CZAR	TOZE	ZYGA
	DAZE	TREZ	ZYME
Z – 2–letter words	DOZE	TUZZ	
ZO	DOZY	TZAR	
	DZHO	VIZY	
Z – 3–letter words	DZOS	WHIZ	
ADZ	FAZE	ZACK	
BEZ	FIZZ	ZAGS	
BIZ	FOZY	ZANY	
COZ	FRIZ	ZAPS	
CUZ	FUZE	ZARF	
DZO	FUZZ	ZATI	
FEZ			
FIZ			

Z – 5–letter words

S
C
R
A
B
B
L
E

ABUZZ	DAZER	IZARD	PIZZA
ADZES	DAZES	IZZAT	PLAZA
AGAZE	DIAZO	JAZZY	POZZY
AIZLE	DITZY	KANZU	PRIZE
AMAZE	DIZEN	KARZY	PUZEL
AVIZE	DIZZY	KAZIS	PZAZZ
AVYZE	DOZED	KAZOO	RAZED
AZANS	DOZEN	KLUTZ	RAZEE
AZIDE	DOZER	KRANZ	RAZES
AZINE	DOZES	KUDZU	RAZOO
AZOIC	DZHOS	LAZAR	RAZOR
AZOTE	FAZED	LAZED	RITZY
AZOTH	FAZES	LAZES	RIZAS
AZURE	FEEZE	LAZOS	ROZET
AZURN	FEZES	LAZZI	ROZIT
AZURY	FIZZY	LAZZO	SADZA
AZYGY	FRIZE	LEAZE	SAZES
AZYME	FRIZZ	LEZES	SCUZZ
AZYMS	FROZE	LEZZY	SEAZE
BAIZE	FURZE	LOZEN	SEIZE
BAZAR	FURZY	MAIZE	SENZA
BEZEL	FUZEE	MATZA	SIZAR
BEZES	FUZES	MATZO	SIZED
BLAZE	FUZZY	MAZED	SIZEL
BLITZ	GAUZE	MAZER	SIZER
BONZA	GAUZY	MAZES	SIZES
BONZE	GAZAL	MAZUT	SPITZ
BOOZE	GAZED	MEZES	SQUIZ
BOOZY	GAZER	MEZZE	TAZZA
BOZOS	GAZES	MEZZO	TAZZE
BRAZE	GAZON	MILTZ	TEAZE
BRIZE	GAZOO	MIZEN	TIZZY
BUAZE	GHAZI	MOTZA	TOAZE
BUZZY	GIZMO	MOZED	TOPAZ
BWAZI	GLAZE	MOZES	TOUZE
CAPIZ	GLAZY	MUZZY	TOUZY
CEAZE	GLITZ	MZEES	TOWZE
CHIZZ	GLOZE	NAZES	TOWZY
CLOZE	GONZO	NAZIR	TOZED
COBZA	GRAZE	NEEZE	TOZES
COLZA	GRIZE	NIZAM	TOZIE
COZED	HAMZA	OOZED	TZARS
COZEN	HAZED	OOZES	ULZIE
COZES	HAZEL	OUZEL	UNZIP
CRAZE	HAZER	OUZOS	VEZIR
CRAZY	HAZES	OZEKI	VIZIR
CROZE	HEEZE	OZONE	VIZOR
CZARS	HERTZ	PEAZE	VOZHD
DARZI	HIZEN	PEIZE	WALTZ
DAZED	HUZZA	PIEZO	WANZE
	HUZZY	PIZES	WAZIR

46

WEIZE	ZIMBS
WHIZZ	ZINCO
WINZE	ZINCS
WIZEN	ZINCY
WOOTZ	ZINEB
WOOZY	ZINGS
ZABRA	ZINGY
ZACKS	ZINKE
ZAIRE	ZINKY
ZAKAT	ZIPPO
ZAMAN	ZIPPY
ZAMBO	ZIZEL
ZAMIA	ZLOTY
ZANJA	ZOBOS
ZANTE	ZOBUS
ZANZE	ZOCCO
ZAPPY	ZOEAE
ZARFS	ZOEAL
ZATIS	ZOEAS
ZAXES	ZOISM
ZEALS	ZOIST
ZEBEC	ZOMBI
ZEBRA	ZONAE
ZEBUB	ZONAL
ZEBUS	ZONDA
ZEINS	ZONED
ZERDA	ZONES
ZEROS	ZONKS
ZESTS	ZOOEA
ZESTY	ZOOID
ZETAS	ZOOKS
ZEXES	ZOOMS
ZEZES	ZOONS
ZHOMO	ZOPPO
ZIBET	ZORIL
ZIFFS	ZORRO
ZIGAN	ZOUKS
ZILAS	ZOWIE
ZILCH	ZULUS
ZIMBI	ZUPAN
	ZUPAS
	ZURFS
	ZUZIM
	ZYGAL
	ZYGON
	ZYMES
	ZYMIC

Bonus words

The 50–point bonus awarded for playing all seven tiles in one move makes seven- and eight-letter words particularly attractive when playing Scrabble. A successful way to learn seven- and eight-letter words is to focus on common six-letter groups of letters (stems) plus an additional one or two letters. *Official Scrabble Lists* shows 250 six-letter stems ranked in order of usefulness in Scrabble. These stems are then shown, with a mnemonic as an aide-mémoire, as an alphabetical listing of 6–plus-1 sets (to form seven-letter words) and 6–plus-2 sets (to form eight-letter words).
To give an idea of how these stems can be put to use we show the top ten of the seven-letter sets.

7–letter sets

AEINRT 1
(RETAIN)
BATEBRIN
CCANTIER
CERTAIN
CREATIN
CRINATE
NACRITE
DDETRAIN
TRAINED
ERETINAE
TRAINEE
FFAINTER
FENITAR
GGRANITE
GRATINE
INGRATE
TANGIER
TEARING
HHAIRNET
INEARTH
THERIAN
IINERTIA
JJANTIER
NARTJIE
KKERATIN
LENTRAIL
LATRINE
RATLINE
RELIANT
RETINAL
TRENAIL

MMINARET
RAIMENT
NENTRAIN
TRANNIE
OOTARINE
PPAINTER
PERTAIN
REPAINT
RRETRAIN
TERRAIN
TRAINER
SANESTRI
NASTIER
RATINES
RESIANT
RETAINS
RETINAS
RETSINA
STAINER
STARNIE
STEARIN
TINTREAT
ITERANT
NATTIER
NITRATE
TARTINE
TERTIAN
URUINATE
TAURINE
URANITE
URINATE
WTAWNIER
TINWARE

AEINST 2
(SATINE)
ATAENIAS
BBASINET
BESAINT
BESTAIN
DCANIEST
CINEAST

CDETAINS
INSTEAD
SAINTED
SATINED
STAINED
EETESIAN
FFAINEST
NAIFEST
GEASTING
EATINGS
GAINEST
GENISTA
INGATES
INGESTA
SEATING
TANGIES
TEASING
TSIGANE
IISATINE
JJANTIES
TAJINES
KINTAKES
KENTIAS
TANKIES
LEASTLIN
ELASTIN
ENTAILS
SALIENT
SLAINTE
STANIEL
TENAILS
MINMATES

MAINEST
MANTIES
TAMINES
NINANEST
OATONIES
PPANTIES
PATINES
SAPIENT
SPINATE
RANESTRI
NASTIER
RATINES
RESIANT
RETAINS
RETINAS
RETSINA
STAINER
STARNIE
STEARIN
SENTASIS
NASTIES
SESTINA
TANSIES
TISANES
TINSTATE
SATINET
UAUNTIES
SINUATE
VNAIVEST
NATIVES
VAINEST
WAWNIEST
TAWNIES
WANIEST
WANTIES
ZZANIEST

AEIRST 3
(SATIRE)
AARISTAE
ASTERIA
ATRESIA
BBAITERS
BARITES
CCRISTAE
RACIEST
STEARIC
DARIDEST
ASTERID
ASTRIDE
DIASTER

DISRATE
STAIDER
STAIRED
TARDIES
TIRADES
EAERIEST
SERIATE
FFAIREST
GAGISTER
GAITERS
STAGIER
STRIGAE
TRIAGES
HHASTIER
SHERIAT
IAIRIEST
IRISATE
KARKITES
KARITES
LREALIST
RETAILS
SALTIER
SALTIRE
SLATIER
MIMARETS
MAESTRI
MAISTER
MASTIER
MISRATE
SEMITAR
SMARTIE
NANESTRI
NASTIER
RATINES
RESIANT
RETAINS
RETINAS
RETSINA
STAINER
STARNIE
STEARIN
OOARIEST
OTARIES
PPARTIES
PASTIER
PIASTRE
PIRATES
PRATIES
TRAIPSE
RARTSIER
SERRATI

TARRIES
TARSIER
SARTSIES
SAIREST
SATIRES
TIRASSE
TARTIEST
ARTISTE
ATTIRES
IRATEST
STRIATE
TASTIER
TERTIAS
VTAIVERS
VASTIER
WWAISTER
WAITERS
WARIEST

ADEINR 4
(RAINED)
AARANEID
BBANDIER
BRAINED
CCAIRNED
CARNIED
DDANDIER
DRAINED
FFRIANDE
GAREDING
DEARING
DERAIGN
EARDING
GRADINE
GRAINED
READING
HHANDIER
IDENARII
MADERMIN
INARMED
OANEROID
PPARDINE
RDRAINER
RANDIER
SRANDIES
SANDIER
SARDINE
TDETRAIN
TRAINED
UUNAIRED
URANIDE

VINVADER
RAVINED

EIORST 5
(TORIES)
AOARIEST
OTARIES
BORBIEST
SORBITE
CEROTICS
TERCIOS
DEDITORS
ROISTED
ROSITED
SORTIED
STEROID
STORIED
TIERODS
TRIODES
FFOISTER
FORTIES
GGOITERS
GOITRES
GORIEST
HHERIOTS
HOISTER
SHORTIE
TOSHIER
IRIOTISE
KROKIEST
LLOITERS
TOILERS
MEROTISM
MOISTER
MORTISE
TRISOME
NNORITES
ORIENTS
STONIER
TERSION
TRIONES
OOORIEST
ROOTIES
SOOTIER
TOORIES
PPERIOST
PORIEST
REPOSIT
RIPOSTE
ROPIEST
RRIOTERS

ROISTER
RORIEST
SROSIEST
SORITES
SORTIES
STORIES
TOSSIER
TSTOITER
UOURIEST
TOURIES
TOUSIER
VTORSIVE
WOWRIEST
TOWSIER

AEINRS 6
(SARNIE)
CARSENIC
CARNIES
CERASIN
DRANDIES
SANDIER
SARDINE
FINFARES
SERAFIN
GANGRIES
EARINGS
ERASING
GAINERS
GRAINES
REGAINS
REGINAS
SEARING
SERINGA
HARSHINE
HERNIAS
ISENARII
JINJERAS
KSNAKIER
LNAILERS
MMARINES
REMAINS
SEMINAR
SIRNAME
NINSANER
INSNARE
OERASION
PRAPINES
RSIERRAN
SNARIER
SARSINES

SARNIES
TANESTRI
NASTIER
RATINES
RESIANT
RETAINS
RETINAS
RETSINA
STAINER
STARNIE
STEARIN
VAVENIRS
RAVINES

EINORS 7
(SENIOR)
AERASION
CCOINERS
CRINOSE
CRONIES
ORCEINS
ORCINES
RECOINS
SERICON
DONSIER
INDORSE
ROSINED
GERINGOS

IGNORES
REGIONS
SIGNORE
HHEROINS
INSHORE
IIONISER
IRONIES
IRONISE
NOISIER
JJOINERS
REJOINS
LNEROLIS
MMERINOS
MERSION
OEROSION
PORPINES
PIONERS
PROINES
RIRONERS
SORNISES
SENIORS
SONERIS
SONSIER
TNORITES
ORIENTS
STONIER
TERSION
TRIONES

S
C
R
A
B
B
L
E

49

UURINOSE
VRENVOIS
VERSION
WSNOWIER

EEINRT 8
(ENTIRE)
ARETINAE
TRAINEE
BBENTIER
CENTERIC
ENTICER
ETEENIER
FFEINTER
GGENTIER
INTEGER
TEERING
TREEING
HNEITHER
THEREIN
IERINITE
NITERIE
KKERNITE
NINTERNE
PINEPTER
RINERTER
REINTER
RENTIER
TERRINE
SENTIRES
ENTRIES
NERITES
TRENISE
TNETTIER
TENTIER
UNEURITE
RETINUE
REUNITE
UTERINE

AENRST 9
(ANTERS)
AANESTRA
BBANTERS
CCANTERS
CARNETS
NECTARS
RECANTS
SCANTER
TANRECS

TRANCES
DENDARTS
STANDER
STARNED
EEARNEST
EASTERN
NEAREST
GARGENTS
GARNETS
STRANGE
HANTHERS
HARTENS
THENARS
IANESTRI
NASTIER
RATINES
RESIANT
RETAINS
RETINAS
RETSINA
STAINER
STARNIE
STEARIN
KRANKEST
STARKEN
TANKERS
LANTLERS
RENTALS
SALTERN
STERNAL
MARTSMEN
MARTENS
SARMENT
SMARTEN
NTANNERS
OATONERS
SENATOR
TREASON
PARPENTS
ENTRAPS
PANTERS
PARENTS
PASTERN
PERSANT
TREPANS
RERRANTS
RANTERS
SSARSNET
TRANSES
TNATTERS

RATTENS
UAUNTERS
NATURES
SAUNTER
VSERVANT
TAVERNS
VERSANT
WSTRAWEN
WANTERS
YTRAYNES

AEILRT 10
(RETAIL)
BLIBRATE
TABLIER
TRIABLE
CARTICLE
RECITAL
TALCIER
DDILATER
TRAILED
EATELIER
REALTIE
HLATHIER
KTALKIER

LLITERAL
TALLIER
MLAMITER
MALTIER
NENTRAIL
LATRINE
RATLINE
RELIANT
RETINAL
TRENAIL
PPLAITER
PLATIER
RRETIRAL
RETRIAL
TRAILER
SREALIST
RETAILS
SALTIER
SALTIRE
SLATIER
TTERTIAL
UURALITE
WWALTIER
YIRATELY
REALITY

Scrabble, like any other game, is honed and refined by those who play it. At the end of the book you'll find a number of variations of standard Scrabble that have been developed. In the next chapter four actual games are described move-by-move to show Scrabble as it is played at the highest level. And here four of the leading players focus their thoughts on some of the fundamental skills that have helped them move up the rankings from average Scrabble players to champions. Their thoughts first appeared in a series of articles in *Onwords*, the leading UK Scrabble magazine for the last fifteen years, and I would like to repeat my thanks to all of them, in particular Allan Simmons, editor of *Onwords*, and Terry Hollington, articles editor of *Onwords* and the player who masterminded the APSP ratings system, for making it possible to share them with a wider readership here.

John Holgate

Teach Yourself Scrabble Vocabulary

A medical librarian from Sydney, John Holgate is one of the leading Scrabble players in Australia. As well as winning top events in Australia, John is also an international player having made his mark at several of the major North American tournaments and the World Championships. He has written extensively about Scrabble and today is a key member of the Australian Scrabble Players' Association.

To the keen Scrabble player, acquiring word knowledge is as basic to expert play as the memorizing of openings and combinations is to the masters of chess. The Scrabble player's tactical skills – `sight of the board', rack management, opening and closing strategy, endgame finesse, counting tiles – and the ability to anagrammatize are all dependent on word power. Of course we have all come across players with a dictionary-like intelligence but little tactical skill, and others who make brilliant use of their natural vocabulary. In the long run, though, the Scrabble player who knows that VARIOLE takes an O, that DENTURES contains three anagrams, and the SHTCHIS isn't really a bad rack, must have an advantage. The sheer logodaedaly exhibited by top players these days can be quite perplexing to the neophyte bumbazed by a plethora of Scrabble. How can he or she build a store of words which will improve scoring potential? How do the `experts' acquire words? What mnemonic devices are there which will help a player to recall letter combinations when faced with a `weird and wonderful' rack?

In attempting to answer these questions, I have outlined a simple and systematic approach to increasing word power.

The development of a sound Scrabble vocabulary does not come from some cabbalistic communion with *Chambers*, nor an osmotic absorption of OSPD. It is built up by adding to your own personal active and passive word knowledge in the following ways:

1   **The Bower Bird Technique**

You pick up words from your opponents as you play. This is the `simplest method; the more you play (and the more erudite your opponents), the more words you pick up. An unusual nine-timer, a challenge or a play that wins a game (or a tournament) will often etch a word indelibly on your memory, but writing down unknown words played against you is a more systematic method. A trap for the `bower birds' is the player who deliberately feeds them illegal words in the middle of a tournament (`I just played TEARINGS for 131!'). Other variations of bower-birding are: kibitzing, borrowing other players' lists; listening to post-game analyses; skimming through *Onwords*; adjudicating; and playing with an open dictionary (in club or solo play). It is important to bower birds to check all words they pick up. One player I know always challenges an unfamiliar seven-letter word to `fix it in my mind', but when the same word later appears on her rack she can never remember the result of the challenge.

2   Serendipity (finding words by `happy accident')

The most common form of this method is simply browsing through the dictionary (that's how I found that Serendip is an old name for Ceylon). It does require a certain amount of spare time but reading definitions helps fix words in the memory. Other forms are doing crosswords, reading widely, and attempting to solve the puzzles in *Onwords*. Exponents of serendipity often play words that are in every dictionary except *Chambers*, have a weakness for the exotic (rather than high-scoring) words, and like to give the full-blown definition of a word while waiting for the challenge slip (like the second meaning of GETTER, or the only meaning of MERKIN). Going to bed with *Chambers* is yet another way of improving your vocabulary (but maybe not your love life).

3   The Rote Method (mechanical memory work)

Fluency in Scrabble (just like any other language) demands a fair amount of conscious memorization. Some players compile lists, some make use of computer files or word processors, others record words on tapes, playing them back using a walkman by day and a headphone for subliminal absorption by night.

Joel Wapnick, the 1983 North American Champion, `rehearses' 1200 words each day whilst walking his dog, brushing his teeth, and driving a car (about forty minutes in all). They are actually guide words to a myriad of sublists (for example, SATIRE, RETINA). In the 1970s Neil Cartledge (a former Australian champion) memorized the *Concise Oxford* by using a card system in a unique way. While driving a cab he regularly pinned guide words to the reverse side of the sun flap and could glance at the cards between fares. Some players adorn the small room in their house with mnemonic graffiti and attach a ball-point pen to the toilet roll holder. These days there is an abundance of published lists based on *Chambers*, and these can be used as a basis for your personal file (notebook, card system, or word processor).

When revising write down two-letter combinations (AD, OO, EL, etc) and test your knowledge of letters before and after (BAD, BOO, BEL etc; ADD, OOP, ELL etc). Gradually you develop a short list of twos and threes that give you trouble (e.g. CEP, KEB, TYG). My strategy for learning the fours was to list them in four groups –

- Those extending to sevens (ACHY, AIRN, BABY etc).
- Those which are extended threes (ABAC, ADIT etc) not in group 1.
- High-scoring fours not included in groups 1 and 2 (e.g. FYKE, ZYME)
- Blockers, dumpers, and fours to go out with (e.g. UNBE, URAO, VOAR).

The initial listing contains no words that are in your active vocabulary (including their extensions). As with the twos and threes, a short list is developed after each revision.

A similar system also applies to the five-letter words, but with the sixes, sevens and eights we move into bonus territory, where a more sophisticated method of memorization is needed.

4   Anagrams and Paradigms (recall by association)

Why do some new words stick in our minds

when others will not? Certain words can have a haunting idiosyncrasy, a memorable association, or they can be thoroughly bland and forgettable. We remember words like DYBBUKS, NOCAKES and HAIDUKS because of their eccentricity, words like NICOTIANS and RINGBONE because they are Toscanini and Borgnine in disguise. We forget SABELLA, INULASE and TENAILLE. We need to create associations for unfamiliar words by building a network which links the unknown to the known. A famous Russian idiot savant remembered everything said or read to him by imagining he was a postman and his memory was a town. Each bit of information was `posted' and recalled by retrieving it from the numbered letter-box of each house – all he had to do was wander around the town until he found the right street and house number. Fortunately no-one tried to teach him Scrabble. But his principle of putting things in context still applied; SABELLA gains in memorability as `ISABELLA minus an eye', INULASE can be seen as `U surrounded by ALIENS' and TENAILLE is LINEATE plus L. Some players do have excellent visual memories. Marie Knight, for example, tends to recall the position of her words on particular pages of the dictionary. In the 1981 New South Wales Championship her opponent tried to impress by giving the definition of a challenged word. `Yes', Marie replied, `it's on page 1460 at the top'. The incident was related to the editor of *Chambers* and was alluded to in the preface to the 1983 edition (page vii, first paragraph). All players, even with `photographic memories', need to regularly practise the three R's – Recordation, Recall, Revision. There are various methods of developing systems of association – each player has to decide which suits him or her.

a   **Anagrams** – do make lists of words which contain one or more anagrams (for example, STIPULE/PULIEST/PUTELIS). *Chambers Anagrams* provides a very useful starting point for personal lists.
    When Allan Simmons's excellent anagram dictionary of sevens with the basic tiles first appeared I spent twelve months memorizing each word and testing myself by identifying the anagram(s). It gave me the ability to spot any seven with the basic tiles (seventy-five per cent of the total) and I'd recommend the exercise to all who aim at fluency in Scrabble. I later prepared a similar list of `basic' eight-letter words. That part of my mind once used for daydreaming (whilst travelling on a bus or watching a boring soap on TV) became absorbed in anagrammatizing random letter clusters (... ORSTINU ... OUTRINS? ... UNROIST? ... – of course, NITROUS and TURIONS!). One should be aware of the danger of verbigeration though. I once partnered Neil Cartledge in a tennis match. As he was about to serve in the first game I asked him `What's the anagram of EGIBONS?' Our game soon went to pieces as we kept on shouting BIGNOSE! BINGOES! SOBEING! etc. etc. to the amusement of our opponents who won 6–2, 6–1, 6–0.

b   **Combos** – combinations of six or seven letters which yield a bonus by adding a letter (e.g. SATIRE + A – ASTERIA, ATRESIA etc., CRINATE + A – CARINATE etc.). Gyles Brandreth, Mike Goldman and Esther Perrins [née Byers] have each published lists of combos [and now there is *Official Scrabble Lists*]. Brandreth's listing is a good starting point. Jim Warmington and Barry Harridge are preparing a comprehensive Combo-6 listing (with index) – interestingly SATINE and SINGLE are the most fruitful 6-letter combinations. Revision is generally done by self-testing: SATINE + A? SINGLE + K? INGOES + Y? It is also good to list (and remember) the letters which don't combine to form a bonus (e.g. SATIRE + J, Q, U, Y, Z).

c   **Nests** – eight- or nine-letter words yielding sevens or eights with the deletion of a letter. If, for example, you have an unplayable SEMINAL (or MENIALS) with a usable G on the board, you might see MALINGERS which contains nine bonus combinations with each deletion of a letter

(MALINGERS – R = MEASLING). Other nine-letter nests are IDOLATERS, ATROPINES, ORDINATES and TRIANGLES. Useful eight-letter nests include MINARETS, REACTION and LIBRATES.

d **Vowel paradigms** – arranging seven- and eight-letter words, with four or five vowels, into a mnemonic pattern. This method is popular in America and was described by Joel Wapnick in the *Scrabble Players Newspaper*, April 1982. Since words with four or five vowels are often hard to remember (and to find on your rack) he prepared lists of words according to vowel sets (e.g. AAAAI – ARAPAIMA, ATARAXIA; AAAEI = ACADEMIA; AAAEU – AQUACADE; etc.)into groups of approximately 200 words containing ten subsets of twenty. The first word of each subset and group formed a cue word enabling him to memorize each group. By memorizing twenty new words at a time (about the optimum number for retention) in five-minute sessions, and each day `rehearsing' (or revising) 1,200 previously memorized words. Wapnick was gradually able to spot sevens or eights in tournament play by identifying a vowel set. Most of us would tend to exchange when confronted by AAAAI etc., but this unique method often enabled him to `squeeze a bonus out of a pimple'. Initially though, he used to practice rack management in reverse and end up with some useless racks of low-scoring vowels. If you find this method daunting you might use it selectively – say for the 250-odd words containing five vowels, or the sevens and eights with three As or three Os, etc.

e **Memory tricks** – devices to improve retention and recall.

   ◼ Guide words – use the key word of the sets you are memorizing to trigger recall. It may be the base word of a combination (SATIRE, CRINATE etc.) or an acronym of the initial letters of each word in a set. Sometimes a formula is handy. When recalling the fifteen eight-letter words with AEIOU, I say to myself `A3 C D2 E4 J M O P S' – triggering the list ABOIDEAU, ABOITEAU, AGOUTIES, CAESIOUS, DIALOGUE, DOULEIAS etc.

Giving a pattern to the list is helpful, or combining the words in a story. For example, SATIRE + P = `PASTIER PIRATES TRAIPSE off to PARTIES and pay a PIASTRE for their PRATIES'. Or to recall all eights with AAOO – `A Swiss JACKAROO, tired of shouting HALLALOO at a KANGAROO and a WALLAROO, hired a MASOOLAH (or MASSOOLA) and took a BOATLOAD of AVOCADOES to the South Sea islands in search of his AMOROSA. He wandered amongst the COOLABAH and MAKOMAKO trees then picked WOORARAS and listened to the TAPACOLO bird. There he found his love, perfumed with OPOPANAX, and gently strummed his GAZOOKA. "You PALOOKA with a BAZOOKA" she exclaimed, "You cantonal CACAFOGO with TOXOCARA!" But when he told her he had written an APOLOGIA, for a PARAZOON, her heart was won and they lived happily ever after on OOLAKANS and MACAROON.' (Based on an idea by Al Weissman in *Scrabble Players Newspaper*, April 1982).

   ◼ Many players prepare lists (and sub-lists) which contain a common feature or theme. For example:

1 All sevens and eights containing J, Q, X, Z.
2 Names of people and places (VANESSA, MAXWELL, CANADA).
3 Sixes or sevens which take a letter either before or after (EVIRATE/LEVIRATE, AXILLA/MAXILLA, STAMPED/STAMPEDE)

5 Consonant genealogy

To memorize the sevens containing the basic tiles (A E I O U/D G L N R S T) plus one mid-value tile (B C F H K M P V W Y) I have developed a system of consonant sets starting with various combinations of D G L N R S T.

The `family tree' of the RST set, for example reads:

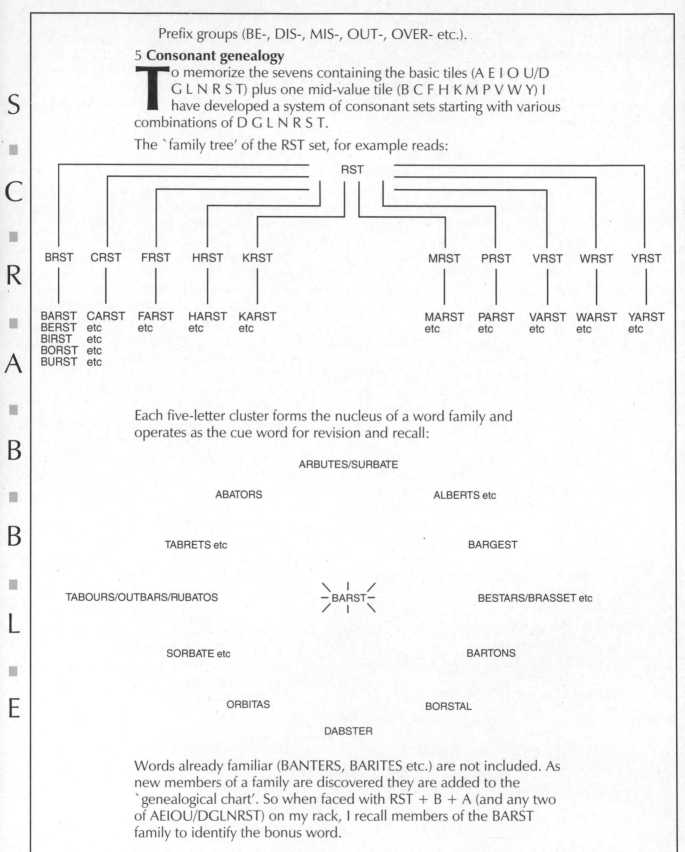

Each five-letter cluster forms the nucleus of a word family and operates as the cue word for revision and recall:

ARBUTES/SURBATE

ABATORS   ALBERTS etc

TABRETS etc   BARGEST

TABOURS/OUTBARS/RUBATOS   –⚬BARST⚬–   BESTARS/BRASSET etc

SORBATE etc   BARTONS

ORBITAS   BORSTAL

DABSTER

Words already familiar (BANTERS, BARITES etc.) are not included. As new members of a family are discovered they are added to the `genealogical chart'. So when faced with RST + B + A (and any two of AEIOU/DGLNRST) on my rack, I recall members of the BARST family to identify the bonus word.

6 Permutations – words linked by changing a single letter

Another way to learn sevens and eights is to collect, and then memorize, `permutation clusters'. My favourite is the `MORONIC permutation' of twenty-two adjectives ending in –IC and containing M or P:

MORONIC MONODIC MONADIC (NOMADIC)
DEMONIC TONEMIC NEMATIC ENTOMIC
ENTOPIC (NEPOTIC) METONIC TOTEMIC
MITOTIC MEIOTIC SOMITIC OSMOTIC
SOMATIC POTAMIC PTARMIC PIRATIC
PAROTIC PROOTIC

Generally clusters of ten or less are best for recall. One I have found most useful is the Z-words permutation ZANIEST, ZELANTS, ZEALOTS, AZOTISE, ZOISITE, OOZIEST, OZONISE, ZOONITE, ZOOLITE, ZEOLITE.

These then are some of the techniques you can use to become proficient in the noble art of Scrabble. Often you will not notice immediate rewards in general play, and it takes some months for your patiently acquired stock of new words to filter down into the great creative unconscious where bonuses are born. One player I know spent five years trying to play CONIINE and when he finally `got it down' he formed an illegal three-letter word and lost the challenge (and the only spot for his word).

The fun of developing a network of Scrabble words can be almost equal to that of actually playing the game and, as every Scrabble player knows, there is always that magic moment when one's personal CONIINE, after hiving in the tile bag for many summers, finally buzzes across the board.

Russell Byers

S
.
C
.
R
.
A
.
B
.
B
.
L
.
E

Russell Byers was the National Scrabble Champion in 1982 and 1989. In 1994 he became the British Matchplay Champion having taken thirteen out of seventeen games to win the title. This success was followed by a semi-final place in the 1994 National Scrabble Championships when he was narrowly beaten to a place in the final by the eventual winner, Mike Willis.

Here he looks at the particular role each letter of the alphabet plays in Scrabble.

Letter Analysis

We all know that certain letters have their role in the English vocabulary but below is my own analysis of the usefulness of each letter in relation to Scrabble.

A   Useful with high-scoring tiles and for bonuses.

B   Best for starting words – watch out for A-hook in front of some words. e.g. ABEAM, ABACK, ABLOOM.

C   Good blocking letter when words begin with C – good for unusual bonuses – goes well with E, H, K, N.

D   Needs an E to be useful – best for single letter extension at end of words.

E   Best vowel, most common letter in words but only the third best vowel for high-scoring tiles.

F   Best use for starting words. Not bad in third position of bonus words but must rely on certain letters – RE or IN.

G   Goes well in any letter position except second. Relies on certain other letters – ING or AGE.

H   Very useful tile all round – First, second or fourth position in words very common. Watch for S-hook in front of some words.

I   Weak against high-scoring tiles but good for bonus plays.

J   Best use for starting, concentrate mainly on short words, relies heavily on certain letters for long words.

K   Best for short words – useful with C, E, N.

L   Relies heavily on high-scoring tiles for short words and low-scoring tiles for bonuses.

M   Quite a common letter – best use to start a word.

N   An excellent consonant – goes well with a number of letters C, G, K, T. Not so good with L.

O   Best vowel for scoring tiles, only fourth best for bonuses.

P   As with M, a common letter – best use to start a word or in third position.

Q   Needs a U to be useful – Watch out for S-hook in front of some words, e.g. SQUIT, SQUAT, SQUIRT.

R   With the exception of S, most useful

consonant – good in any position of word but relies somewhat on an E.

S Best letter available – best use at single letter hooks in front of or at the end of words.

T Very useful consonant – good in any position except second.

U Relies on Q with another vowel – serves some purpose with other high-scoring tiles.

V Needs an E. Best to start a word (the ideal blocker) or second from last in longer words – VE ending.

W Good with vowels A, E, O, for two-letter words – relies on low-scoring consonants.

X Best use next to vowels – For longer words an E is the most useful accompanying letter.

Y Good for two-letter words – relies on L or R in long words.

Z Very useful letter – needs an E or O – concentrate mainly on short words.

From the analysis above I set below the order of letters relating to their usefulness divided into three sections as it is very difficult to compare a useful lower-scoring consonant to a high-scoring letter.

1 pointers – S E R T A I N O L U

2 to 5 pointers – H M P D G K W C Y B F V

8 to 10 pointers – X Z J Q

Brian Sugar

Brian Sugar is a legal clerk and has been playing Scrabble for twenty years. He has won many tournaments and was runner-up in the National Scrabble Championships in 1981. A member of the APSP committee, Brian is the author of numerous articles on Scrabble. Here he gives some matchplay advice.

The First Rack

The opening rack is unique, faced with the empty board you have the advantage of first blood and the opponent will be put under immediate pressure to neutralize the lead. The initiative should not be given away lightly.

It follows that it is rarely good to exchange tiles on the first turn but an exception might be to exchange the Q rather than play QAT when holding A E N Q R S T since A N T E R S is likely to yield a bonus on the next play. Serious Scrabble players will be well aware of the riches obtained from any of the R E T A I N S six-letter combinations.

Important considerations are the more obvious placing of a high-scoring tile on a double-letter-score and avoidance of placing a vowel adjacent to a premium square right down to less obvious thoughts of setting up a `four-timer', the risk of a suffix or prefix extending to the triple-word-score and, even, the bonus possibility of an eight-letter word being trebled in score. (An E on the star spot is much more vulnerable than, say, an O!) Not the least consideration is tile turnover. You are much more likely to draw the coveted blanks if you use fifty-plus tiles, than if using rather less than fifty. It is that simple, yet tile turnover is often quite unappreciated as an important tactic of the game.

G A C E U L E – This was my opening rack playing against Gareth Williams in the 1990 Prestige. I debated between GLUE or LUGE, GLACE, GUE or LEAGUE and finally opted for GLACE. I was not very happy about the rack leave of U E, mainly because a U is such an obstacle. Although Gareth was happy about the choice of GLACE, I now believe that LEAGUE (starting d8) not only gave a better tile turnover but, also, that the remaining C would have gone with an O and L pick-up for COLLEAGUE (36 points) next turn.

O V A A I P H – Here the choice is between OPAH, OVA or PAH. OVA is far too ambitious. I think OPAH is best with a reasonable rack leave of VIA. (When you have several high-scoring tiles it is often worth retaining one – as next turn's scoring insurance.)

G U M L E K S – If the words are in your vocabulary the choice is between MUSKEG and MUSKLE. Otherwise, the plays are ELK, GUM, GLUME or KEG. GLUME at d8 for a reasonable turnover (and gets rid of the U) but the rack leave of K, with S, would not be that wonderful.

F R A D O I C – You could take some time over this one. Using the two high-scoring letters it is difficult to find a suitable five-lettered word play. I would opt for FOCI – keeping R A D, the best rack leave.

C L O N A R T – It would be too risky to change L (going for a bonus just because CARTON goes with all the vowels except the A). I would opt for either CANTOR or CARLOT, giving CANTOR the edge since there are more Ns than Ls. I would not play COL keeping R A N T because this would rely on a lucky pick-up. However, if the rack had been....

C L O N A S T – Play COL keeping S A N T ...

It makes a big difference when you already hold the S, you can then go for a far more ambitious play! Incidentally S A N T is a better leave than L A S T – so playing COL is preferred to CON.

E E T R E T U – You might think of TRUE or UTTER – but the play should be TUTEE, keeping E R the best leave.

A L D L O E U – Nearly all `one-pointers' so it has to be worth offloading tiles. There are many choices, DUELLO, ALUDEL, ALLUDE but I prefer ALOUD leaving one vowel and one consonant.

It should always be borne in mind that even if your vocabulary is more limited than you would like, a moment's thoughtfulness on the placement of your tiles, or the rack balance, could significantly change your game for the better. Retaining a playable word – on its own – is probably an acceptable balance, it does not have to be an equal number of consonants and vowels! Finally – don't go for turnover when the only plum in the pudding is a sour Q.

FINEST SELECTED FRUIT

Allan Simmons

Allan Simmons is one of the finest UK Scrabble players, the victor of numerous competitions and one of the consistently highest ranked players in the APSP ratings. For the Scrabble movement as a whole his most significant contribution is as the founder and editor of *Onwords* which has taken Scrabble news and views to players around the world since its first issue in July 1980. You can read about *Onwords* in greater detail later, for the time being here is Allan offering guidance on: playing to win; bonus building; rack-balancing; and tile-tracking.

Playing to Win

The strategy for `playing to win' is not quite as simple as getting the highest score each turn whilst doing as much damage to the openings. Playing for scores alone a player is not at all concerned with the opponent's score, and the game is really a matter of both players playing against the luck of the draw. The situation is quite different when winning the game is the only objective. Your opponent's score relative to yours is what determines more than anything how you should play the game. If you're winning the game you want to stay in front, if you're losing you want to catch up, and if it's really `eye for eye, tooth for tooth' you want to get the edge. Pretty obvious really, but each situation dictates a different approach. The important thing is to keep control of the game, and this applies from the word Go. Let's look at some hypothetical board positions and the sort of winning strategies that might be used. Remember, these are not rules but merely ploys to bear in mind, since rules will always have exceptions.

Situation 1: Empty Board – your move

If you have no vowels, no consonants, the Q and no U, or the makings of a bonus, then the best time to change is now. A rack that could be considered to have the makings of a bonus would be something like: ADEGNSV or AAEORST. In both cases it is likely that your opponent will score more if you play a word than if he goes first, especially with the second rack. If you change and your opponent plays, then you will have useful floaters and more scope for a bonus word. With the examples the best letters to keep are ADENS and AERST.

If your rack dictates that you play a word first move then bear the following in mind: unless you benefit considerably from using the double-letter premium it is safer to play a three- or two-letter word. With ADDEGOT, DOG would be a safer move that GATED, but with DELONUW. WOULD's score could be considered enough to outweigh its openness compared to, say, WUD. When you play the word, wherever possible, make sure that the vowels are not next to the premium squares as it only invites an easy score for the opponent. If you have to play vowels next to the premium squares then I and U are preferable to A, E or O because of the number of playable two-letter words. The ideal words to play are those that take few letter extensions, remembering that it is often easier to see extensions at the end of a word than it is to the beginning. Likewise, it's easier for your opponent to see scoring possibilities if you play the first word horizontally than if you play it vertically. That's because we're used to reading from left to right rather than downwards. In about ninety-eight per cent of all games first moves are played across, so confuse your opponent and play down.

Situation 2: Behind by 100+ points

As this situation is obviously different depending on the stage of the game I've divided the following into three parts: the early game, the mid-game, and the end-game. Firstly, a general bit of advice – never give up.

The Early Game: This situation generally occurs when your opponent starts with a bonus or two when there's little you can do to prevent it. Often this will mean that the board has become quite open. You have a choice – adopt a policy of blocking all dangerous openings or continue to play a `cautious' open game to get the bonus that you need to catch up. You must decide on your policy and stick to it. It's no good wasting good letters to block the board, assuming you can catch up over the rest of the game, then getting an S and making a useful opening. Your opponent could be lurking on the brink of a bonus, just waiting for that vital opening. If you reckon that you are better than your opponent at `bonusing' then it's better to strive to keep the board open. It is useful if you are adept at seeing eight-letter words because you can then open the board by providing floating eighth letters rather seven-letter openings which are easier for weaker players to

use. If you're not a bonus person then ruthless blocking is the only answer. This also applies if your opponent is as good as you at getting bonuses down.

The Mid-Game: If you're behind considerably at the mid-game stage then it's a little late to adopt a policy of blocking. In fact, your opponent would rather you waste your good letters to block the board and save him the trouble because after all, he's way out in front. You really need a bonus to catch up and you can't rely on luck to provide a place to go when you do get that bonus. How do you create openings that your opponent won't take? First, examine the board for existing openings. Make a mental note of any useful extendable words that your opponent appears to have missed in previous plays. Perhaps he doesn't know the word – a useful situation to be in because you have a `safe' place to play a bonus and can afford to force your opponent to waste letters to block the openings you make elsewhere on the board. The only bonus possibilities on a mid-game are often eight-letter words. So it is often a good ploy to forego a seven-letter opening if you can get a reasonable score for doing so and provide yourself with floaters. Whenever possible, make openings by playing words that take letter extensions that you have remaining on your rack. Towards the end of a game a quick count of the vowels could reveal that, for example, with the rack AEGINOT, GO may be a good play because you have A and E for AGO/EGO and there are no other As or Es left.

The End-Game: I reiterate here, never give up. I remember playing Brian Sugar in the Club KO in 1979. I was 100 behind and had the rack EFIINRS on the last pickup. There was only a -Y ending on a triple and I didn't chance RESINIFY for 95, which would have won the game. I didn't play it because, as a team we couldn't risk losing a go and the vital points. In fact we won the match, 6–all and by 50–60 points. So the message is: a) a bonus worth 100 points could easily crop up on the last rack and fit into the only available place, and b) if you're in a team and assume that you've lost the game, still play to maximize your score and minimize your opponent's.

Situation 3: Playing a Bonus

If you find that you have a bonus on your rack at an early stage of the game you will probably find that it will go down on the board somewhere. A frequent mistake, though, can be to disregard the strategy of winning play and put the bonus word in the first place without examining the board for alternative positions. Similarly, an alternative bonus might be a better play. The fact that a bonus play brings in an extra 50 points, possibly putting you some way in front as a result, doesn't mean that you shouldn't take the same considerations into account as you do when playing the tighter, non-bonus words. Bear in mind what you are giving away to your opponent – your aim is to give the minimum of scoring opportunities away, even if it means sacrificing a few points yourself. There may even be the situation when only one possible bonus play is available and, if you're in front, the best move is for you *not* to play the bonus – especially if it opens the board and there is a chance that your opponent has a blank or S.

Assuming you need to play a bonus and you have a bonus word on your rack, consider the following:

- If you have a choice of playable words in the same position then consider how easy it might be for your opponent to extend the word for an easy high-score or bonus play. A non-extendable seven- or eight-letter word is generally the best play, but especially avoid playing an -S extendable word if it is in an open position. However, an -S extendable word played into a restricted area, even if it does give a triple-word square to your opponent, may tempt him to use an S for a relatively low score.

- Consider how many letters will be available as floaters for an eight-letter word once your bonus is played and, particularly, how usable they are. For example, try to avoid leaving the commoner letters open.

- Avoid leaving vowels next to the premium squares, especially the triple-letter squares where your opponent might easily obtain 28+ points for words such as AH, KA, AX, IF, ZO etc. played in parallel. Most importantly, the vowels O, A and E, and less importantly I and U. Priority must also be given to the tiles J, X, Q, Z – make sure they are not available next to double- or triple-word squares.

As you are primarily concerned that your opponent doesn't reply to your bonus play with a bonus him/herself, the order of importance of the above strategic points is as listed, 1, 2, and 3. Be especially wary of giving away bonus possibilities if you have noticed that your opponent has been showing the usual signs of having a good rack with bonus potential – typically, using one tile at a time after a lot of thought, tile shuffling, or wasting an S for a pitiful score (possibly a duplicate, then again it might just be bad play!). It could be said that a good player will give more away on the sort of rack he has than a poor player.

Bonus Building

[During the 1970s and 1980s there was a trend in the UK to play Scrabble openly for high scores. Today the emphasis is on the matchplay winning style. Bonus building skills complement both styles of play.]

Are promising six-letter combinations really worth keeping? It takes an experienced player to decide when and when not to play that single tile in the hope of producing a bonus word the following go.

A seventy per cent chance of a bonus is not a certainty. Remember that most of the good six-letter combinations given in Scrabble books are not necessarily that good once tiles have been played. They are based on the chances of picking up letters at the start of the game. A lot of apparently good combinations like RETING and LISTER are also dependant on there being a reasonable number of vowels left in comparison with the awkward consonants that are left.

The game is not just about bonuses. It is about

scoring as well. It is easy to become obsessed with playing bonus words and keeping those six-letter combinations but it's fatal to fall into the one-letter-at-a-time trap.

So break up the six-letter combination by playing more than one letter.

What does this do for you?

It gives you more choice of what to play.

It is likely to give you a higher score than one tile would do.

It increases your chances of picking up any good tiles still remaining.

Aim to have a six-letter combination on your rack after the next pickup by keeping the basic five- and four-letter groups that are the backbone of six-letter combinations and being aware of the common tiles you are likely to pick up.

For example, keeping ANTER or INTER could lead to RETAIN the next go.

The secret is to be aware of what vowels are likely to appear on your rack since your aim is to avoid duplicates and keep a balance.

So learn how many of each vowel there are in the set and count the vowels played. It will help you decide whether to play the A, I or E from your rack to keep ANTER, INTER or TRAIN for example. So think in terms of five-letter or even four-letter combinations.

The following diagram of the RETAINS family shows how four- and five-letter groups can lead to several different six-letter combinations.

Some more useful five-letter combinations (without Ss) that form the basis of many bonus words are:

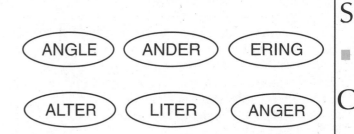

One last point, if you think you're one of the unlucky ones who never gets good letters on which to build bonuses – How many times do you change?

Rack-balancing

In any game of Scrabble, whether playing for high scores or wins, you will have a wider choice of moves each turn, and be more likely to have a bonus word, if your rack is balanced. A wider choice of moves gives you more control over what tiles you keep, which in turn should lead to a balanced rack the following go, and so on.

But first, what is meant by a balanced rack? There are forty-two vowels and fifty-six consonants in the set, plus the two blanks. Ignoring the blanks, the ratio is four consonants for every three vowels and it is that ideal balance that you should be aiming for on your

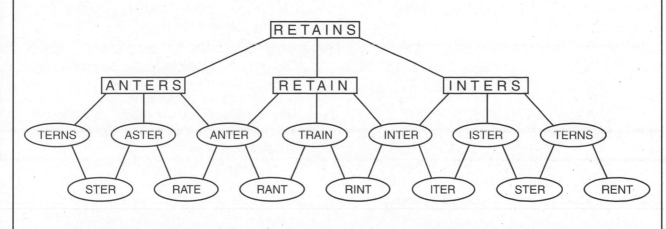

rack. In practice though, a rack with three consonants and four vowels or even five consonants and two vowels can be nicely balanced if the letters fit together.

From that it can be deduced that an unbalanced rack is going to be one that has too many vowels or too many consonants. No medals for working that out! But what also constitutes an imbalance is more than one of the same letter whether it be a consonant or vowel. So a rack might have an ideal 4–4 balance but it is not so promising if the tiles are: GGVTIIA. An all too familiar rack, perhaps? Why is it, I heard you ask, that the top players never seem to suffer from similar bad racks? Well, believe me they do, but they are often able to limit the suffering by resolving the problem as early as possible before the rack deteriorates. Indeed, some of the skills of Scrabble are recognizing a problem rack, knowing what to do with it, and of course, having that specialized vocabulary to match. But wouldn't it be nice if those bad racks didn't occur so often? After all, prevention is better than cure.

So how does one prevent?

Generally, you need to keep the letters that are more likely to leave you with a balance on your rack after your next pickup, bearing in mind the distribution of letters left at any stage of the game. That sounds like too much hard work initially but there are some shortcuts and, in practice, it is not something that is necessary every move. Some games flow better than others and some racks have more obvious solutions than others.

You need to be aware of the following distribution facts:1) The Consonant–Vowel ratio of 4 to 3 (C–V ratio) 2) The number of each vowel in the set: E-12 A-9 I-9 O-8 U-4 3) The number of each common consonant: D-4 L-4 N-6 R-6 S-4 T-6

And you need to apply that information during the game. It is very easy to overlook the fact that the initial distribution is constantly changing during play. The balance of vowels

and consonants that remain, and the sort of vowels and consonants they are, is information you can glean from observing the tiles already played. And this is very useful information for decision making:

■ A choice of which vowel to play –

Count up each of the vowels. Determine which one you are likely to pick up. Consider that your opponent may well have an A, E and I on their rack and include that in your count. If vowel usage is on par, play your most awkward vowel.

e.g. HIAONRT: Count As, Is and Os to decide on playing HA, HO, or HI.

■ Indecision of whether to play or change that extra tile – check the C–V ratio, it will make the decision for you.

e.g. GGVTIIA: (Assume you wish to change). Definitely change GGVI but what to keep out of TIA? Count Ts, Is and As. Don't keep TA if too many As left. If the C–V ratio is favouring consonants, consider keeping TIA. If too many vowels are left then consider just keeping the T. If there are not many Ts out then why not change the lot!?

■ Whether to keep a promising six-letter combination or not – ·

Many six-letter combinations combine with the vowels to make seven-letter words but it is wise to check the C–V ratio once you get to mid-game.

e.g. A combination like STORED may drop in value as EALING increases! (STORED fits well with the vowels, and EALING fits well with the consonants – try them.)

e.g. Don't be afraid to break up your RETAIN combination. First, consider which of the letters of RETAIN you are likely to pick up.

■ Don't forget the game is about compromise, and there are times when the score for a move might outweigh the imbalance that is left. But if that is the case then you can't complain about your next rack.

Tracking Techniques

Tile-tracking is the recording of tiles played during a game for the purpose of advising the player of unplayed tiles. This is standard practice amongst regular tournament players in most Scrabble-playing countries although some (New Zealand for example) do not allow it.

Most players instinctively practise a very crude form of tile-tracking when they mentally make a note of key letters played or general observations; the Ss and blanks have gone, the Q is to come, there's only one U left, there are not many Es out, both Hs have gone, and so on.

Whilst tile-tracking has been practised for many years across the Atlantic, in the UK the use of pen and paper to tile-track really took off with the establishment of the matchplay tournament circuit. The early APSP playing rules permitted tile-tracking, but no prepared checklists were allowed so players had to use their game time to establish such lists. However, a few years back the rule was relaxed to allow prepared tile-tracking sheets. This has extended to the National Scrabble Championships where, since 1990, the official scoresheet has featured a preprinted tile-tracking grid.

So tile-tracking is allowable but why do it? What are the benefits?

Many players painstakingly tile-track every game without perhaps realizing the full benefits. Tile-tracking just to determine what the opponent has on the rack at the end of the game is only really fulfilling one objective, albeit an important one. There are other uses for tile-tracking which can improve a player's overall performance.

Knowing remaining tiles at *any stage* of the game enables assessment of:

■ Likely pickups –

There are ten vowels and twenty-five consonants left so from a rack of IIAAOHG keeping three or four vowels ought not to be too bad because you are likely to pick two or three consonants.

Only the one and two-point tiles are left so, if behind, a possibility of a bonus may be viable.

Most of the awkward higher scoring tiles are left so be aware of keeping back vowels to give flexibility of use should you pick them.

■ Probability of picking specific tiles –

With the rack IAAOHRG (above) you note you have the last two As so no danger in keeping them both. Or, you note there are plentiful Ns left so playing HOA may be more favourable than AGIO because of the potential -ARING combination.

■ Opponent's likely rack –

The remaining letters are AAEEIIKLNNORRSTTVW – your opponent is likely to have a bonus.

The remaining letters are AAAAAIKLNORSTVVWWY – your opponent is likely to have two As, and perhaps a V or W or both.

There is no real bonus threat unless the opponent's last play was suggestive of this.

As any game progresses so the more informative the tracking and the greater use it has. It is a decision-making tool for:

■ Finer bonus-probability calculating –

The combinations PARDON and VEWERS both go well with vowels and not much else. If behind and the letters remaining are vowel-heavy then the bonus possibility is worth considering.

You have RETAIN but the letters left are AAAEIOQRUVVXYYZ – the odds are not so high after all.

■ Winning endgame strategies –

The scores are level and your last rack is BUCKSOO and your opponent has GENOTVX. You work out there is one VOX-scoring danger which you can only block with OO for 4 although BUCKS scores you 30 in two different places. You play OO first.

■ Advising when high turnover is wise –

You have the Q and no U and there are two Us left.

The two blanks are left.

- ■ Or unwise –

There are fifteen left, the Us have gone, the Q is still out, and your opponent just changed.

- ■ When to go for broke –

You're 90 behind with AOOECIA and there's a one in ten chance of a Z for ZOOECIA so you use the spare A to set up a 100+ bonus play.

- ■ And when to stay coolly in control –

The Q is left and you have AABSTUV and a score of 40 is available for TUBAS. But you have the last two As and are able to play VAST to give an unblockable (A)VAST on a triple and keep the U.

If you don't practise tile-tracking then you may wish to consider introducing one of the variety of tracking methods to your game. If you already practise tile-tracking then you may want to experiment with a slightly different method and attempt to use it in different ways.

However, if your only objective is to determine the opponent's last rack it can be just as straightforward and perhaps more reliable to wait until the twilight of the game and then spend a minute or so establishing remaining tiles. If you tile-track throughout the game just to achieve this then there is scope for mid-game mistracking giving the wrong conclusion and you having to re-check anyway.

The more popular techniques of tile-tracking are outlined next.

Countup

This is straightforward. The letters of the alphabet are written down on a sheet and a mark is placed against each letter as one is used. When there are none of a letter left the letter is crossed off. This is easy to set up but is not as clear as the `Countdown' method (below) because it does not provide at-a-glance information on the number of tiles remaining. Perhaps the players who use this method do so as a hangover from the days

when establishing the tracking sheet had to be done in their own game time.

Countdown

A large number of players opt for this method. This involves writing the letters of the alphabet down the sheet and against each letter a mark for each occurrence of that letter in the set. A variation of this is to replace the mark with a `countdown' of numbers.

As letters are used the numbers (or marks) are crossed off enabling the player to read off the number of that specific tile remaining.

Set-List

The `Set-List' is as supplied on the National Scrabble Championships official scoresheets and is simply a list of every letter arranged in alphabetical order in a box.

This is more visual than any of the other methods but has the disadvantage that it becomes difficult to extract information quickly as the game progresses and the grid becomes cluttered.

Grouped Set-List

This technique involves listing every individual letter as for Set-List but arranging them in groups according to letter type. The actual groups chosen may vary from player to player. Some may just separate out the vowels and consonants and others may further split up the consonants. This is my trusty method and one which I find most readily provides the information needed during play for making strategic decisions quickly. A sample layout representing a part-complete game is shown here.

```
A A A    A A A    A A A
E E E E  E E E E  E E E E
I I I    X X X    X X X
O O O O  O O O O
U U      U U

J Q  X Z K
S S  S S  [?]  [?]
B B  G G G  N N N N N N
C C  H H  T T T X X X
F F  M M M  R R R R R R
V V  P P  D D D D
W W  Y Y  L L L L
```

Since a priority is to have at-a-glance information about remaining letters, even this method can become visually ineffective half-way through the game. The solutions are either to encircle remaining tiles so as to highlight them (see sample below), or to write them out again separately, retaining appropriate groupings. The danger with the latter is that some letters can easily get missed out in the transposition. However, when down to the last dozen or so (excluding one's own rack). I normally do this anyway. Always double-check at this stage and preferably in your opponent's thinking time.

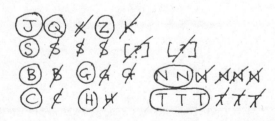

But will YOU benefit?

Tile-tracking is not essential and if you are not comfortable or disciplined enough to tile-track, or it becomes a distraction and your normal game suffers as a consequence then you are better off not doing it. However, you are urged to allow a period of acclimatization if the technique is new to you – you will get it wrong many times before it becomes consistently useful to you. Whatever, you should try and set aside some time towards the endgame to establish/confirm the last few letters left unless, of course, you are confident you are going to win without endgame letter knowledge.

Russell Byers

Ten Tips To Improve

Following his success at the 1994 APSP British Matchplay Championship, Russell was asked for a few tips and came up with these which help to round-up the previous ideas and suggestions made by him and the other three leading players.

Russell Byers won thirteen out of seventeen games to take the title at this year's APSP British Matchplay Championship and followed up this success with a semi-final placing at the National Scrabble Championships, narrowly beaten by Mike Willis for a place in the final. *Onwords* asked Russell for a handful of tips for lesser Scrabble mortals and he dutifully obliged....

1 Word Power

I feel it is largely up to each individual as to how much learning should be done as each player has their own capacity level where over-learning then degrades recall.

Given that all Scrabble players are reasonably familiar with a sufficient range of shorter words with JQXZ and the routine seven-letter words, it seems that there is likely to be scope for improvement on difficult seven-letter words and eight-letter words formed from non-bonus combinations.

For example, some seven-letter words that I have learnt specifically and played on a number of occasions are: GLUTAEI, LINGUAE, AIERIES, RIPIENO.

Some eight-letter word sets I have learnt for non-bonus racks and again, have proved useful include (note only a few words are instanced for each set):

PANTOES + 1:
SAPONITE, PENTOSAN, TEASPOON
HANTIES + 1:
ASTHENIA, ABSINTHE, THESPIAN
IRELAND + 1:
DRAGLINE, HARDLINE, INLANDER
RETONES + 1:
SERMONET, ONSETTER, OVERNETS
NETTIES + 1:
TEOSINTE, ANISETTE, INEPTEST
OTERIES + 1:
ETAERIOS, TROELIES, ESOTERIC
TRINODE + 1:
DORMIENT, CENTROID, INTORTED

2 Use of the S

I would not advise holding on to an S until a bonus comes along. Using your only S to block a bonus position for 25–30 points is reasonable providing you are also turning over five or six tiles in the process to increase chances of picking up more of the better letters.

3 Use of the Blank

Unless the blank is helping get rid of the Q for 30–40 points or more, I would not advise using the blank for less than 50 (endgame excepted).

4 Time Control

It is important not to rush your opening move if you are going first. The best move may not be obvious. Once into the game, try and make time by playing one or two of the more obvious moves swiftly to keep ahead of time and aim for at least five minutes left going into the endgame (two or so tiles left in the bag).

5 Board Control

Without conceding too many points try and make your opponent play in specific places on the board so that you have other areas for your own benefit. A prime example is `baiting' access to a central tws when you have bonus potential. If the opponent takes the bait and plays to the tws it will provide floaters for eight-letter plays.

6 Block or Open?

Do not worry about the board being too open if you are scoring well each move. A couple of good back-to-back scores of 30+ is equivalent to a bonus. You need to ensure there are two separated openings if you are significantly behind. Conversely you need to block if you are 40 to 60 points ahead.

7   Changing

If in doubt about changing a certain letter, change it. Don't be afraid to score zero in one move since it is better than struggling for a few points for each of the next few turns with an ever-worsening rack. Changing will (hopefully) give you back control of the rack.

8   Letter Distribution

Keep a watch for any unusual letter distribution with the unseen tiles: imbalance of vowel/consonant ratio; abundance of high-scorers left; many of a particular vowel left; only low-scoring letters left, etc.

9   Endgame

It is imperative to leave at least one tile in the bag when scores are close and you have the option to do so. You are more likely to play out first which could make a difference of 30 points and swing a close game in your favour.

10   Psychology

If you are playing a superior player don't convince yourself you have lost before the first word is played! Any reasonable player has potential to beat anyone. If you have read these tips and put them into practice you will increase your chances of beating top players.

LIVE SCRABBLE®

Inside top players' minds

One of the most instructive and rewarding ways of improving your Scrabble, as with most other sports and games, is to learn from more experienced players. Annotated games, like the ones featured here give a unique insight into what goes through the minds of top players as they ponder their racks, study the board, keep track of their opponents' letters and sort through their well-drilled vocabularies for the right word.

Here are four championship games, three from the UK National Scrabble Championships of 1992, 1993 and 1994, and one from the 1993 World Scrabble Championship.

Each game is described move by move and each move gives details of the player's rack, the word played in that move (or the change of letters), the position of the word, the number of points scored by the move and the player's total number of points in the game.

All of the games came from the final matches of the four competitions, played under the spotlight (literally) and in front of cameras relaying the game by closed circuit television to the audience in another room. In these circumstances the pressure on both players is intense and it is understandable when they don't always spot the optimum moves picked up by the annotators who enjoy the benefit of calm reflection after the game has ended. On the other hand when a player plays an inspired move, the tension generated by final match conditions make such a move even more outstanding.

You can follow the games as they develop, playing each move on your own board to get a feel of what it is like to win (and lose) a major championship title.

The notation used is easy to follow:

Positions of plays are shown by column (a–o), by row (1–15) and either across (a) or down (d).

Blank titles are designated `?'.

Double Letter squares are abbreviated to `dls'.

Triple Letter squares are abbreviated to `tls'.

Double Word square are abbreviated to `dws'.

Triple Word squares are abbreviated to `tws'.

1992 NATIONAL SCRABBLE CHAMPIONSHIPS – FINAL

Pete Finley versus Philip Nelkon

The 1992 final gave me the chance to become National Champion for the fourth time. My opponent in the best-of-three final was Pete Finley from Sunderland. Pete ranks as the leading player from the North-East of England who has consistently appeared in the top ten ratings of the Association of Premier Scrabble Players, of which he is one of the principal figures.

I won the first game in the final and the one described here was the second which Pete had to win to keep alive his Championship chances.

Dick Chinnery, a seasoned Scrabble commentator who regularly annotates games for *Onwords* adds his own thoughts to Pete's and mine.

Pete Finley

Philip Nelkon

	rack	move	pos	score	total
1	AAEEEFV	change 6		0	0

Finley: Almost fell for EAVE but remembered in time that you can't have just one. No real alternative but to change.
Chinnery: The only reasonable alternative to changing is VAE (f8a) leaving the imbalance of AEEF. This avoids revealing the rack problem to the opponent and provides a 12-point advantage. It is unlikely the VAE play will give away more than Nelkon would otherwise score on an empty board (plays such as AX (f9a) are not possible). However, the greater turnover and likely rack balance achieved by changing 6 is of greater value than the 12 points scored.

	rack	move	pos	score	total
2	E AIIORU	EUOI	f8a	8	8

Finley: No printable comment!
Chinnery: The options are really change again keeping

	rack	move	pos	score	total
1	AAILOOS	change 3		0	0

Nelkon: My choice was between changing 6, keeping the S, or changing just 3, keeping SAIL. I have had past success holding SAIL and this attracted me given the likelihood of floaters to play off next turn.
Chinnery: The change by Finley and the weak scoring options available to Nelkon (eg OLIO e7a) make changing a must. As Nelkon points out he has even more of an advantage over Finley with his change because of the possibility of floaters from Finley's next play. Holding on to the SAIL balance is probably better than chancing on a random draw by changing 6.

	rack	move	pos	score	total
2	AILS AO?	ABOuLIAS	g5d	59	59

Nelkon: Could only find ABOuLIAS. rOSALIA probably

ER, play EUOI (f8a), or play AUREI (say, at g8a). Nelkon's change of 3 suggests a promising rack. The few points scored for EUOI or AUREI are not that relevant in the decision making for Finley. The dominating factors are rack leave, availability of floaters, availability of the initial dws, and tile turnover. A logical analysis serves to demonstrate how a decision could be made by allocating marks for the moves being considered.

	EUOI	AUREI	change AIIOU
score	1	1	0
floaters	2	1	3
rack	2	1	3
dws	2	2	0
turnover	1	2	2
board control	1	1	0
	= 9	= 8	= 8

Obviously, individuals may allocate different weightings but my analysis agrees with Finley's choice.

3   AIR EEGT   AEGIRITE   d10a   65   73

Finley: Four possible positions for AEGIRITE. i5d is most defensive but I was in an attacking frame of mind at the time.
Chinnery: As Finley points out, an attacking choice. The E left at k10 and the flexible AEGIRITE(S) hook could be considered unnecessarily open. My choice would have been the defensive play from i5d.

4   BLNOPRT   PORN   b11a   18   91

Finley: My assumption that the previous move left us one tws each backfired somewhat. Could have played TORN (h12d) for the same score but the BLP leave didn't appeal.
Chinnery: PORN (or even BORN) removes dws at e11 and –S bonus likelihood along row 12 but generates scope for a high-scoring dws play from the dls at a12. Given the vowel shortage extra turnover may be more beneficial. PROBE (f4d for 25) is better in that respect. However, my preference would be to keep the balance and restrict the openings created by AEGIRITE with PLEB (k8d for 16).

5   BLTELOY   OBEY   h12d   33   124

Finley: Could have scored more for TOBY at a12a but was concerned that I was falling behind and the board was closing. I wanted floaters at the top and bottom of the board so went for the h12d spot. TOBY would have been a better rack leave, but I preferred the floating E left by OBEY.
Chinnery: I seem to recall that one of the assistants at the NSC, London League player Tamsin Rawlins, pointed out that this rack made POTBELLY with the P at h1a. An

better but only opens up one tws (didn't see it at the time).
Chinnery: Possible bonuses apart from those two are ALOgIAS (d7a) and ASOcIAL (i7a). rOSALIA (f7a) scores the most (67) but the low 59–67 points range for any of the bonus plays suggests that positioning rather than score should be an overriding consideration. The two tws openings created by ABOuLIAS would give it an advantage over the others which all open up just one high-scoring tws position.

3   ADEFPTY   PEATY   h1d   38   97

Nelkon: Wasn't sure of FAYED. PEATY suited me nicely.
Chinnery: In the same position: FAYED avoids leaving the floating E and scores more (42); TYPED (39) keeps a better balance (FA) but the T is a dangerous eight-letter ending (-IEST); ADEPT (35) keeps the useful FY back but leaves the ADE floaters. The extra points for FAYED and the potential of the PT leave over FD probably makes it the best move.

4   DFERSTV   STERVED   k5d   44   141

Chinnery: The best play for turnover, score, and defence.

5   F GNQRSW   change FGNQW   0   141

Nelkon: This hand looked pretty impossible at the time but with only one U gone, WIRING (i7d) for 19 now looks like a better move.
Chinnery: How about a WRONG move (e7a) for one more point? The highest scoring play is SWARF (d8d) for 24 but is devalued because it uses the S, retains the Q, and creates openings. Playing rather than changing keeps the pressure on Finley and doesn't reveal the problem

excellent find and a possible play if double-challenge applied in UK (the word is in the American OSPD but unfortunately not in OSW). Whilst acknowledging Finley's reasons for opting for OBEY, I would add value to the rack balance of ELL and the ARY(L) scoring possibility created with the TOBY move (a12a). However, most attractive because of turnover and E retention is TALLBOY (g3a for 28). It opens a little but it also takes out floating A and E of PEATY. Another high turnover play is EYEBOLT (h2a for 28) but it would be foolish to leave the O at 12 and the –S hook on a tws column.

| 6 | LLTEFIU | LIFE | a12a | 31 | 151 |

Finley: I confess I didn't see FUTILELY – which is odd, because I considered the –FULLY ending and dismissed FLUTILY as unlikely. I was happy to capitalize on Nelkon's change and take the lead for the first time, albeit briefly.

Chinnery: An unfortunate miss by Finley. An alternative for LIFE is FUTILE (l3d) for 2 less points but higher turnover.

| 7 | LTU INNW | WONT | f7a | 18 | 173 |

Finley: I wanted to play TWIN (c13a) but wasn't sure of AREW (I always said I'd be dangerous if I knew all the fours!) I wasn't happy with WONT but couldn't really see anything better.

Chinnery: UNWIT (b2a for 24) achieves the turnover necessary with a weak rack like this and takes out the tls danger at f2. The score for TWIN probably outweighs those factors considering it too would remove a scoring threat.

| 8 | ILNU FIN | FUNNILY | b15a | 14 | 187 |

Finley: Falling behind again and a bad rack to boot. Had to have a clear out. Funnily enough, I spotted the perfect place.

Chinnery: The best strategic play, particularly with a blank to play for. It would be nice to keep the F for c13 scoring but INULIN (a2a) is too dangerous.

rack – a psychological advantage on top of the score advantage.

| 6 | RS ECHWX | EXARCH | f3a | 27 | 168 |

Nelkon: I was pleased with this move – it took out some of the bonus potential around rows 2 and 3, gave turnover, and created scoring spots for both of the letters left on my rack.

Chinnery: Although utilizing much of the wealth of the rack in one turn, a skilful creative play not untypical of Nelkon. The highest scoring play is EX (i2d for 36) but this leaves an imbalanced rack that may not yield other scoring possibilities for the high-scoring tile retained. For those of us who might not spot the EXARCH option, WAX (g3a for 25) of CHAY (e5a for 24) are lower-scoring, less-turnover solutions that leave powerful racks of CHERS and WERSX respectively.

| 7 | SW EEIMT | WISE | l1d | 41 | 209 |

Nelkon: Considered WIMPIEST (b8d for 42) but thought adjective was probably only WIMPISH. WEE (f2a for 36) is good, retaining the S but not taking out any bonus opportunities. Chose WISE for score but feel in retrospect WEE may have been better.

Chinnery: EXARCHIES and EXARCHIST are possibilities but both are more open than WISE. TWEE (e2a) is a setup for the tws access (ST) and the (E)TWEE hook. Does Finley know the latter? Such a play would probably draw suspicion because of the needless T played and could force Finley into rack-damaging defensive play along row 1. This could be an advantage but if Finley leaves it alone the EXARCH(S) and (E)TWEE openings become a subsequent dilemma for Nelkon. Stick with the WEE move which also leaves a bonus potential rack with E at h14.

| 8 | EMT DMRZ | MEET | f14a | 24 | 233 |

Nelkon: Rejected ZED (f2d for 33) in preference to attempting to cut down bonus opportunities on rows 13 and 14. MEET is a weak move. TREZ (k6a) is probably better.

Chinnery: Holding onto the E and grabbing the extra points for ZED is tempting but TREZ may be even better because it takes out the easy bonus hook onto the E at m4. However, given the fact that Finley has had a random pick of 6 tiles the bonus openings are not topmost priority, and with only two other Es left it may be wiser to give weight to the E retention and play ZED (f2d).

9   I AIJOOU   EUOI   k7a   5   192

Finley: OUIJA never occurred to me. I wanted to hold the J back for a possible score, and I managed to persuade myself that Philip might fall for EUOIS. It seems rather a vain hope now but I was convinced at the time!
Chinnery: OUIJA (b2a for 32) is indeed the best move.

10   IAJO HST   WHOA   l1a   30   222

Finley: Should have played HAE (f2a) for 36.
Chinnery: Also retaining the scoring J are TAISH or SAITH (2ba for 45). The open tws at a1 is probably worthwhile given the extra points and turnover. Of those two, TAISH is best because of the fewer two-letter words ending -T.

11   IJST BEU   JABS   d1d   42   264

Finley: Had to go for the score with JABS to get close enough to Nelkon to create a chance of pinching the endgame. There were three times as many consonants to come as there were vowels (including the Q), so I wasn't worried about the rack leave of UITE.
Chinnery: It's comforting when the essential play to get the points leaves a rack compatible with the remaining distribution. There is no contention to the JABS play. BITE (a1a for 29) keeps the S and U but the J could be awkward hereafter with the consonant-heavy bag.

12   EITU AKR   TAK   c13a   30   294

Finley: I was aware of the danger of the n10 spot but couldn't do much about it without opening tws's. TAK kept the score pressure on and left me with useful letters should the Q be picked.
Chinnery: Yes, TAK is an excellent move given score situation and remaining tiles.

9   DMRZ NVQ   change   MRNVQ   0   233

Nelkon: ZED (f2d) still a possibility but decided I was sufficiently far ahead to get better letters whilst retaining the ZED scoring insurance.
Chinnery: I would agree with the change. The ZED score would be a short term gain given the appalling rack leave. It can be better to change whilst in control to secure that control rather than struggle with an ever-worsening rack balance.

10   DZ AEGIO   DIAZO   b2a   38   271

Nelkon: Considered DAZE, GAZE, DOZE from ċ4 but was worried about giving away points at f2 and e4 from the Z. DIAZO gave good turnover although left other opportunities for Finley. I missed the possibility of ZIG (a14a) which, given number of consonants left, would have been best.
Chinnery: Yes, ZIG is best play for 39 points.

11   EG CDGLN   CLOGGED   m5d   14   285

Nelkon: I still think this was the best move although I disliked opening the tls at n10.
Chinnery: The floating O and I bonus possibilities need to be blocked – there is one blank still to appear. Other factors are the rack imbalance, openings created, and titles remaining (AAAEIOU?DKMNQRRTVT). LEG (l14a for 21) leaves dangerous rack imbalance going into the endgame and does not remove bonus dangers. CLOGGED resolves rack problem but creates a scoring danger at n10 (the remaining M is the only real threat). COGGLED (m6d for 14) avoids leaving the n10 danger. Both CLOGGED and COGGLED not only increase chance of getting the blank but also the Q and V. A compromise to be considered is CLOG (m5d for 7) retaining the E and reducing chance of getting the Q. But on reflection the blank may be a greater game decider than the Q. This fact, combined with the comfort of a remaining U and possibilities of QAT and QADI plays, the high turnover and extra 7 points with COGGLED makes it the move that gives best scope for victory.

12   N ADMRV?   DRAY   e5a   16   301

Nelkon: Lucky not to pick up the Q. Didn't know MAViN (n10d for 43) which was undoubtedly the best move. Considered MARDy in same position but was worried about being left with the V. Assuming Finley now has the Q, I saw the greatest dangers to be ROQUE (n10d) and QUAY (e5a). I decided DRAY took out QUAY play but gave 3 more points for QUASI (a4a), but left me with flexibility of the A and blank.
Chinnery: MAViN would have not only scored more but forced Finley to play QUAY or QUASI. The former allows a good score with QUAYD so Finley should respond with QUASI. (As it is known Nelkon picks up the N) Nelkon could then respond with 8 for RID (m13a) and Finley plays out with ORE (o8d for 14) giving Nelkon victory by 2 (335 o 333). Another good scoring play is hADJ (a1a for

13	EIRU AOQ	ROQUE	n10d	39	333

13	AMNV? N	VANs	k15a	21	322

Finley: BARQUE and BAROQUE leap out at me now, but they didn't then. I was just relieved to see ROQUE was enough to win.

Chinnery: That Q is a welcome sight for Finley and any of the words metioned win him the game. The game is played out....

39) but this leaves little scope for endgame victory and Finley wins easily with ROQUE.

14	AI	AI	a14a	14	347

14	MN left

Finley +4 351
Nelkon −4 318
Fortunately the third game went my way.

79

1993 NATIONAL SCRABBLE CHAMPIONSHIP – FINAL

Allan Saldanha versus Karl Khoshnaw

The 1993 final gave the press something particularly special to write about when Allan Saldanha became National Scrabble Champion at the age of fifteen, the youngest in the history of the competition.

Allan's victory was less of a surprise to the Scrabble fraternity, in particular his opponent Karl Khoshnaw, who had first played Allan two years earlier and by his own admission was `thrashed' by him.

Allan started playing Scrabble when he was five and two years later entered the National Scrabble Championship for the first time. In fact his rating among top players of the Association of Premier Scrabble Players at the end of 1992 had already won him a place in the British team heading for the 1993 World Scrabble Championship in New York a few weeks after his victory.

A week before the National Championship Allan had finished sitting nine GCSEs while maths lecturer Karl Khoshnaw had been guiding his students through their exams. Now the two of them squared up for the best of three games, twenty-three years apart in age, but in Scrabble terms worthy opponents. Alone for two hours in an air-conditioned room, watched by four assessors and an adjudicator they battled it out.

Allan won the first game 350–268 and the pressure was on Dr Khoshnaw as they started this second game.

As well as Allan's move-by-move commentary, Dick Chinnery and I add our own thoughts, aided by the 1993 APSP Prestige winner, Andrew Fisher.

With the 1993 World Championship imminent reference is made in the commentary to the *Official Scrabble Players Dictionary* (OSPD), the authoritative Scrabble dictionary in North America, which was to be used in conjunction with *Official Scrabble Words* (OSW) in New York.

Allan Saldanha

	rack	move	pos	score	total
1	INOOTTV	VINT	e8a	14	14

My choice was between VINT and VINO. I preferred VINT as it limited parallel play by Karl. Little to choose between leaves of OOT and OTT.
Chinnery: Agree with VINT over VINO, I prefer keeping

Karl Khoshnaw

	rack	move	pos	score	total
1	BORSTUY	YOB	g9a	26	26

BISTOURY is playable through the I of VINT but tough to find under any conditions, let alone the NSC Final. YOB is probably next best move.

the two Os rather than two Ts. With OSPD there's VON and TOIT with VON being most defensive.

2   TOOERW?   TOW   h10a   21   35

I saw WROOT but did not know it was a verb for WROOTEd. I did not know TOWROpE either so went for TOW which scored nicely and kept OER? (a possible OVER- bonus).

Nelkon: OuTWORE is another bonus – from a10a or j10a would be least dangerous.

Chinnery: kOTOWER (b10a) for 69 is possible with OSPD.

3   OER?EGT   GROVE   e5d   18   53

I considered a play like TOG from j12 but did not like leaving A,E,S, hooks. GROVE scored 18, kept ET?, left two floaters and provided scope for openings later, but leaving little for Karl to score off of.

Chinnery: GROVE is essential to get the board more open if the blank is to bear fruit. Also GREVE.

Nelkon: Given the 90-point deficit I would opt for TOGE because it is more open.

Fisher: Allan needn't panic about falling behind here, the second blank should guarantee a high score at some stage.

4   ?TEADER   REAsTED   m9d   73   126

I considered REAsTED from m9, DEAREsT from m7, GAThERED from e5 and DERATe from d13. The last two were too low-scoring so my choice was between REAsTED and DEAREsT. REAsTED scored 4 less but created two openings, the tls at n10 and the tws's on row 15, whilst DEAREsT only created one so I chose REAsTED, noting that both Bs had gone so no possibility of (B)REASTED.

Chinnery: Not wise to play such an opening move given the luxury of choice although REAsTED is better than DEAREsT (m7d) as Saldanha concludes. Saldanha is not to know of Kohshnaw's weak rack and a 3–letter word play last time by Khoshnaw could easily suggest promising retention. I quite favour GARTErED (e5a) for 68.

Nelkon: DEAREsT for score or GARTERED defensively? I would choose GARTErED.

5   AHIKRTX   XI   n10d   52   178

My choice was between HIKER (j14a) and XI (n10d). HIKER burns more tiles but is more dangerous because of

Chinnery: OUTBY gives best keep of RS but fewer points (possibly balanced by extra two tile turnover). The OUTBY(E) hook created is too generous at this stage perhaps.

2   RSTUCD?   CRUSTeD   e11a   99   125

CRUSTED from e11 is easily the best move and spotted immediately by Karl.

Chinnery: Other inferior bonus plays include: CRUDEST (k5d) 93 and lower scoring CRUDEST/CRUSTED (c11a); CUSTARD (k8d, k7d).

3   ABEEOOP   BAP   j12a   24   149

An unlucky pickup and no easy options. Possible plays are OBOE from f3, BAP or BOP from j12. OBOE leaves the best rack but scores less, replacing G and R floaters of GROVE with O and B. However, I would play BOP (to keep AEEO rather than AEOO), because OBOE leaves a high-scoring opportunity down from g3.

Chinnery: PAEONY restores some balance and blocks floating R and (S)TOTS hook, the P shouldn't be too easy to score with on the tws from h1. Otherwise change must be best. OSPD allows BEEP (j12a) for a few more points and less imbalance.

Nelkon: I would play BOP, agreeing that the change should be delayed.

Fisher: Changing 6 tiles would ensure a paucity of easy openings for Saldanha.

4   OOEEEEI change OOEEEI   0   149

The choice here is changing 6, keeping an E, or playing IDEE (l15a). I would play the latter to keep the pressure on with realistic chances of a two-consonant pickup to ease the rack problem.

Chinnery: Changing may have more logical value by there is hidden psychological advantage in not changing, keeping the opponent guessing about the strength of one's rack. As well as taking the tws, IDEE also reduces the danger. A tls/dws score from j14 I would be a nice choice at this point.

5   EAAJNNS   JANES   j14a   56   205

No alternative to JANES with OSW but with OSPD I might have gone for JNANA/AG (d1d) retaining the S and creating two scoring places, ie the J tws and from c3 down.

the S's to come. XI would put Karl under immediate pressure after his change and I did not feel like passing up 12 points. I also felt that turnover was of secondary importance with both blanks gone, and the XI move still retained scoring potential.

Chinnery: Note the useful H retention for the CH hook at e12. RADIX (k15a) scores 10 points less and blocks the row 15 tws but look how easy that tls/dws row 14 is to use with words such as HOLED or worse still JOLED. OSPD allows KITER, keeping the H.

6   AHKRTAZ   TAK   18d   24   202

Karl's last move blocked a play of HAZARD (h15a) for 60 and left me in a bit of a quandary. I narrowed the choice down to TZAR (17d) and TAK (18d). TZAR scores 11 more, has turnover advantage, but uses the Z. At the time TAK seemed a better option because of Z and H retention and the possibility of an O-pickup giving ZHO (h15a) for 53, however with hindsight I would favour TZAR.

Chinnery: Any play this go must keep back that useful H for the CH hook at e12. Another advantage of TZAR is that any –S bonus play alongside the T will at least give away the top tws whereas this is not the case with TAK.

7   AHRZAIN   RAH   c12a   19   221

A promising rack but surprisingly not many scoring options. The moves worth considering were ZHO (c7a) and RAH (c12a). ZHO was only 6 points more than RAH and used the Z whereas RAH burned an extra tile and kept an excellent AINZ. Under WSC rules NAZI (k5d) provides a good alternative, setting up a RAH play from j4, but the opponent may well take the tls at j6 so this is risky.

Chinnery: Vowel/Consonant ratio is approx 50/50 at this stage. Careful play from this rack should enable Saldanha to stay level with Khoshnaw and retain the scoring Z. Saldanha's play of RAH is about the best score that creates further choice for the Z next turn (an E pickup gives ZAIRE (unpluralizable) from c9). RAH (f14a) for 2 less and same turnover is defensive but could further prohibit Z usage. ARRAH (g10d) for 1 less nicely takes out the easy bonus row 14 with an extra tile turnover.

8   ZAINAHN   HARN   c10d   14   235

Another nice rack with few scoring options. Again I considered ZHO but the leave of AAINN was not encouraging and I didn't want to use both the Z and the H for just 25. I struggled for a while looking for an alternative and finally found HARN (c10d). This again kept the excellent AINZ, kept me in touch with Karl and would force him to open out if he could not play on the tws at a15, possibly creating a high-scoring Z play. An E pickup would enable ZAIRE (b6a). OSPD offers a much better play of HAZAN from a15, putting me way in front and leaving little scoring option for Karl.

6   EANEIMO   MINO   g15a   27   232

MINO is probably the best play if not seeing MEDIA (k15a).

Fisher: MEDIA (k15a) is a stronger move because of the stronger rack leave of ONE, although I enjoyed learning the definition of MINO, `A raincoat of hemp'.

Chinnery: Turnover moves include MEANIE and ANOMIE (k4d) but both leave plentiful openings. OSPD increases the choice with MENO & MANO g15a and MONIE f2d.

7   EAEISUV   UVEA   e14a   21   253

A vowel-heavy rack again but the S may prove important later. UVEA leaves a nice rack at expense of he a15 tws opening. A better play is VAIRE (c9d) for 3 more.

Chinnery: With OSPD, EAVE is allowable doesn't help. VIAE/ET k5d is nice.

8   EISCEFG   ICE   b9d   26   279

ICE at b9, although it scores 26, is much too open and could be very costly. CH can be front-hooked by E, I or O and there are 14 of these letters still to come (from Karl's viewpoint), so the opponent may easily close Karl's 44 point lead next turn. A better play is FECES (a15a) which yields a 53–point lead with higher turnover and no giveaways. OSPD offers a slight improvement on that with FICES, keeping EG in preference to IG.

Nelkon: A poor move with an 18–point lead and a go in hand. Defence and scoring should have been the orders of the day. FECES is best.

Chinnery: An unlucky pickup – an E was probable. Again the board is incompatible with the rack and Saldanha's HARN is a wise choice. The RIZ option is one less turnover but does block the a15 tws usage – any re-use of the Z gives the tws to Saldanha next turn, but that keep of AANNH is not inspiring and would agree with keeping the Z this turn.

9	ZAINEGS	ZIGAN	a11d	60	295

I was fortunate to have the right letters to respond to Karl's opening. This rack makes two bonuses, AGNIZES and SEAZING. I did not recall SEAZING but saw AGNIZES. I recalled playing AGNISED in America and having it disallowed so I doubted AGNIZE being in the English dictionary. Given this element of uncertainty I decided against the bonus because of the high cost of a lost turn. I also wasn't sure of ZIGANS (a4d) so I chose ZIGAN to put me in front, and being comforted by the ES keep.

Chinnery: Saldanha now has a luxury of high-scoring choices apart from the two bonuses. ZIGANS or ZANIES from a4 and ZIGAN or ZINGS from a11 are available. As the 100+ scores of AGNIZES or SEAZING would catapult Saldanha from behind into a 50+ lead here is no advantage in retaining the S (however, as we now know the foregoing of the bonus was not a strategic choice). With OSPD, AGNIZES is playable from k3d.

10	EEFQRSU	QUEERS	k3d	32	327

I was thankful for an obvious move with the Q here that took a bonus place, turnover tiles and left me 26 points in front.

11	FADILNW	DWARF	b6a	24	351

Possibilities I saw were AWFUL (4a), AW (j5d), QADI (k3a) DWARF (b6a). QADI was eliminated because of the

Fisher: This type of open attacking play can sometimes pay dividends, and in the absence of obvious alternatives I might have done the same. The danger is that Allan is almost certain to play down the a-column on this board.

9	ESFGIOO	FOG	a7d	23*	302

Karl is 16 points behind and should look to score off the tws at a8 to re-establish his lead. The best move to achieve this is FOGIES (a4d). The actual play of FOG is probably next best. (*) Note that in the game this was miscounted as 23 when in fact it was worth 24. We realized this after the game but were unable to amend the scores due to the questionable rule that scoresheets could not be altered after the game.

Chinnery: Khoshnaw may have pondered GOOFIES here (non-word). He is 16 points adrift and clearly must take that tws at a8 to score (retaining the S would be nice). Given that the only letters worth keeping are ES but using the S generates an extra 18 points of opponent pressure plus there are many Es to come, retaining the ES is not on balance advantageous. Note that the highest-scoring non-S play, FIGO a6d for 26, is too dangerous because of Y dws/tls danger at b6. Having played FOG next pickup is likely to be something like ELD (a weak non-bonus rack). With OSPD, FOGIE is possible f2d for 26.

10	ESIOIPT	DIP	m15a	20	322

Letters left from Khoshnaw's viewpoint are:

A E E E E I I O O U D D F L L L L M N R W Y

DIP is probably the best move although it only uses two tiles. It keeps Karl in touch and leaves him with a nice rack. Even if the opponent uses the tls at j6, there should be scores available for Karl next turn. EDIT (l15a) is an alternative, scoring 3 more and using an extra tile with OPSD, EDIT is definitely better because of the PE possibility on the TLS at j6 next turn. Playing OPE or OP this go would be dismissed because of the duplicate Is.

Chinnery: Given the little use of the S on the board a high turnover play to go for any of the goodies that are left (U for the Q perhaps Y M or W for the j6 spot) is PITEOUS (e5a) for 20.
Nelkon: There is a need to create counter-play and to try and get some of the high-scoring letters, I therefore prefer PIE (f4d) for 14 points setting up SPIE.
Fisher: Agree, (S)PIE is an excellent set-up and would be difficult to inhibit.

11	ESIOTEE	EGO	d11a	11	333

At this juncture Karl has to decide whether to go all out for a bonus or try to pick up the M, Y or U and score

poor leave and QADI(S) risk and AW eliminated because it only used two tiles and FLIND keep is also poor. AWFUL would block possible QU play and leave IND but would open the tws at h1 and bonus play along row 3. DWARF scored 24, used four tiles with reasonable leave of ILN, blocked G and R of GROVE and restricted bonus use of second E of QUEERS. With OSPD I would have gone for NAW (j4d) for 31, virtually nullifying bonus chances and reducing Q flexibility.

Fisher: A floating L required for WINDFALL from this rack!

Chinnery: Saldanha is just 5 points ahead and has some useful scoring tiles but lacking in vowels. Careful play here could put him in good stead for the endgame, careless play may let in a bonus. Khoshnaw's two-tile play last go may have been priming his rack for a bonus, possibly around the R of GROVE or an E of QUEERS. There is a -Y ending bonus slot on column b and with those Ls left perhaps that is to be treated as a genuine threat. In addition to moves mentioned by Saldanha, I'd quite like DINFUL (g4a) because it sets up FAW next turn but would be mindful of the row 3 bonus openings created. OSPD words include FELID (j6a) and QAID (k3a).

| 12 | ILNOORY | NOY | j4d | 31 | 382 |

Only two bonus plays now left for Karl, MESQUITE and DILUTEES. If I can block both of them, reduce the Q's mobility and score over 15 the game should be mine. The Y allows me several scoring moves of around 30 of which LORY (a4a) and NOY (j4d) are best. I play NOY to block and put me 49 points ahead and, I believe, the game beyond Karl's reach.

enough to win, perhaps by going out first. Karl's move of EGO suggests he has gone for the former as he has played to leave the floaters open. With the remaining letters I can only see possible bonuses of: SLEETIER, SELENITE, MESQUITE, DILUTEES, DETINUES, and RETINUES. All these are extremely unlikely given that there are sixteen unseen letters. It is also likely that the opponent will remove some or all of these floaters. EGO also creates another scoring opening, with six of the sixteen letters left hooking in front of EA. If Karl does not pick up a bonus he is relying on his opponent not having any of M, Y, U or being able to score more than 20. If Karl wanted to realistically go for a bonus he should play FOE (a7a) or OE (b13d) instead as neither opens the dws at d4. However, the best move for Karl would probably be TEE (j5d) in the hope that a U, M or Y pickup would save me. TEE puts Karl 16 behind and the opponent would find it difficult to score without a U or M, the S possibly being Karl's trump card.

Nelkon: I'd play ETUI (i4a) which at least opens two bonus places although the chances of drawing a bonus remain poor.

Fisher: GOE (e5d) might offer better recovery prospects with that final S although the GOE(Y) hooks presents a danger.

Chinnery: Following Fisher's strategy GIO does the trick. With OSPD, FEE e7a making DE is possible but not that helpful.

| 12 | ESITELL | NULL | j4a | 8 | 341 |

Remaining titles from Khoshnaw's viewpoint are:

E E I I O U D L L M R

Karl's only hope of winning now is to play a bonus. His TELLIES is unplayable and there are no openings so he must make a last ditch attempt to create an opening using less than four titles. The actual play of NULL is Karl's S (it also takes an A but they have all gone). It also blocks a Q play but that is incidental. However the opening is obvious and easy to block and with a pickup of any two of the remaining titles left there is only one possible bonus, LEISTER (n1d), so it is highly unlikely that Karl will win the game. Alternative opening plays to be considered are ILEA (d3d), LEA (d4d). YELL (j6a), TEAL (d4d). ILEA leaves no bonus opportunities with any remaining letters and the YELL(S) hook is obvious and easy to block, and only leaves EELIEST as a possible bonus. So the choice is between TEAL and LEA. LEA, with its (I)LEA hook would allow ETOILES, EELIEST and LEISTER, however there are two unseen Is and if the opponent has an I and knows (I)LEA this is easy to block. TEAL would set up (S)TEAL and although the chances of a bonus are reduced (as two letters are played instead of one) it is a lot more difficult

13   **ILORDEI**   **LILO**   **m2d**   8   390

Although I could not see any bonuses with the letters remaining I felt I had to block the opening as it was Karl's only remaining hope. I chose LILO because it reduced use of NULL(S) by Karl. OLID or RILED would have done equally well.

Chinnery: LILIED (m2d) is nice, increasing possibility of a playout next turn.

14   **RDEILM**   **DREAM**   **d3d**   20   410

I saw MERL (a4a) for 24 but this would have given Karl ETUIS (a3a) for 24.

Fisher: REMEAD (d2d) scores a few more, but the difference is immaterial now.

15   **EIL left**

Saldanha −3   407

Khoshnaw +3   369

to block without leaving a floater. Hence I would play TEAL as the shorter of all the long shots!

13   **ESITEEU**   **EE**   **b14d**   10   351

Karl plays off EE to give him two playouts next turn. (EE from b13 scores more).

14   **ESITU**   **SUITED**   **b1d**   14   366

	A	B	C	D	E	F	G	H	I	J	K	L	M	N	O
1	3W	S_1		2L				3W				2L			3W
2		U_1				3L				3L		L_1		2W	
3		I_1	2W	D_2			2L		2L		Q_{10}		I_1		
4	2L	T_1		R_1					2L	N_1	U_1	L_1	L_1		2L
5		E_1			E_1	G_2	O_1			O_1	E_1		O_1		
6		D_2	W_4	A_1	R_1	F_4				Y_4	E_1			3L	
7	F_4		2L	M_3	O_1		2L		2L		R_1		2L		
8	O_1			2L	V_4	I_1	N_1	T_1			S_1	T_1			3W
9	G_2	I_1	2L		E_1		Y_4	O_1	B_3			A_1	R_1		
10		C_3	H_4			3L		T_1	O_1	W_4		K_5	E_1	X_8	
11	Z_{10}	E_1	A_1			C_3	R_1	U_1	S_1	T_1	E^*	D_2		A_1	I_1
12	I_1		R_1	A_1	H_4			2L		B_3	A_1	P_3	S^*		2L
13	G_2		N_1				2L		2L			T_1			
14	A_1	E_1			U_1	V_4	E_1	A_1		J_8	A_1	N_1	E_1	S_1	
15	N_1	E_1		2L		M_3	I_1	N_1	O_1		2L	D_2	I_1	P_3	

1993 WORLD SCRABBLE CHAMPIONSHIP – FINAL

Joel Wapnick (Canada) versus Mark Nyman (UK)

In the words of one commentator, `Game four in the final was quite simply the most amazing game of Scrabble I have ever seen,' and I suspect that few of those who watched it would disagree.

The British team had entered the 1993 WSC better prepared than they had been two years earlier and this was reflected in the final placings. Four British players were placed in the top ten: Clive Spate in ninth position; Allan Saldanha in fifth; Gareth Williams in fourth place: and Mark Nyman who became the 1993 World Scrabble Champion.

There might have been an all-British final if Joel Wapnick hadn't beaten Gareth in the deciding game of their semi-final match.

Joel entered the final as the highest rated player in Canada. The year before he had come second in the North American Open, which he had won ten years previously. A music professor away from the Scrabble board, he is also the author of the *The Champion's Guide to Winning at Scrabble*, published in the USA.

Mark Nyman, a television producer for Channel 4's *Countdown*, took a string of prestigious tournament wins into the match with him. With four Highscore Masters titles to his credit (he gained a fifth on his return from the 1993 WSC), first place in the 1991 Thailand Championship, second place in the 1989 North American Championship and first place in the APSP British Matchplay 1993 he was no stranger to championship Scrabble at home and abroad.

The first of five games was won by Joel Wapnick, in spite of Mark's inspired playing of MUTAGENIC from a rack of ACEGINT. Joel won the second game as well, mirroring the position he had been at in the final of North American Open a year earlier, before he lost the last three games and the championship. So the pressure was on both players in game three. After taking an early lead, Joel slipped behind and the game went to Mark, keeping him in the final with two games to go.

The commentary for the celebrated fourth game comes, appropriately, from Nick Ballard, editor of the North American Scrabble magazine *Medleys*. As both OSPD and OSW words were allowable he marks all OSW-specific words with an asterisk for the benefit of his North American readers.

`It is time to commence Game 4,' Nick wrote, prefacing his commentary, `keep out your board and tiles and play along! If Joel wins, he'll be World Champion. If Mark wins, game 5 will decide.'

JOEL WAPNICK

	rack	move	pos	score	total
1	ADEQSVZ	ZED	8G	26	26

The best play with OSPD. However, with SowPods [OSPD+OSW], ZED's defensive value is reduced (due to ZO*), and Z is a more powerful weapon to keep. Simulation: DEV 8G highest (barely), DEVA 8G –0.5, ZED –1, ADZ 8F –2, ADZE 8G –3.

	rack	move	pos	score	total
2	AIQRSUV	* QUAIR*	D8	48	74

Highest score, and keeps the S. To avoid the UV combo, an interesting (though inferior) alternative is SUQ* J8 (46).

	rack	move	pos	score	total
3	EFIPSUV	FIVES	11C	39	113

Joel spots a nice underlap. It would be desirable to rid the I as well with FIVES at J4, but not for a sacrifice of 6 pts.

	rack	move	pos	score	total
4	AAIJPTU	JUPATI*	K6	30	143

Normally a great play, but here we *know* Opp's rack to be CDIINTU: This play allows Opp PUDIC 8K (33) keeping INT. Our alternative, FUJI C11 also gets us 30 pts, while limiting Opp to DINIC* 11J (25) + an inferior TU leave, a net gain to us of about 12 pts. Offsetting this is FUJI's leave, AAPT, being 6 to 8 pts worse than an AT leave. So, on balance, FUJI is the correct play by about 5 pts (plus

MARK NYMAN

	rack	move	pos	score	total
1	CGIOORU	CURIO	9C	23	23

GUIRO 9C, though 4 less pts, simulated 2.5 pts higher (in spite of the 8A-D opening). GO is a much worse leave than CO, and GUIRO places the I and R better defensively.

	rack	move	pos	score	total
2	ADEEGOT*	DOGEATE*	10F	84	107

The anagram of GOATEED! – second nature if one's home dictionary is OSW. The North American players watching, too, were jumping up and down and shouting this one out.

	rack	move	pos	score	total
3	CDIINTU	"INCUDIT"	7I	0	107

A hushed murmur came over the crowd – could this really be an anagram for DUNITIC? No – Joel's free challenge was successful! Simulation shows DINIC* 11J best, with FUCI C11 at –1 and the crowd favorite DUNITIC K6 at –3.

	rack	move	pos	score	total
4	CDIINTU	IDENTIC	L8	32	139

A cute parallel play, but U is a poor leave. PUDIC 8K (33), with its strong INT leave, iterated 7.5 pts better.

any chance Mark might overreact to what looks like an S setup at 15C).

5   ADEISTV   VISTAED   13B   89   232

Nicely done. SEDATIVE H1 (89), VISTAED M3 (90) and DATIVES M3 (92) score the same or more, but Joel's play looks the most thorough at shutting down bingo lanes.

6   BELRTUY   UBERTY*   A7   54   286

`When you see a good play, look for a better one', Joel bitterly regretted not locking up the title here with BRUTELY or BUTLERY at A6 for 107 pts.

7   BEFLMOR   FORMABLE   N4   69   355

After this move Joel takes a 174–pt lead, and picks his fourth bingo rack in a row. He must have been feeling pretty good.

8   EGHILMN   EHING*   011   41   396

Joel reasoned (at the time) that a 170–pt lead would surely be enough to win. HELMING B1 (83) increases his lead another 42 pts, but risks a triple-triple. Amongst experts watching this incredible game, opinion seemed divided.

9   LMNNORW   MOWN   B4   19   415

Joel later felt he had not taken the possibility of losing this game seriously enough; that he should have simply blocked with OWN 15C, despite 6 less pts and the fourth consonant.

10   AILNNPR   PLAN   1A   21   436

Grabbing points while blocking the most dangerous bingo line. However, even more important than rack leave is to play exactly four tiles; this will leave one tile in the bag for Mark after his bingo (reducing his out-play score while increasing Joel's odds of drawing the H or K for some scoring muscle). In 520 simulations, PLAIN 1A lost only

5   AAALTUY   UVA*   B12   12   151

Simulation: PILAU 8K (21) highest, with YA 14F, AULA M5, ALIYA 13J and UVA at 5–9 pts back. However, cashing the Y at 14F (losing the volatility of a big X-spot and handing Joel row 15), now or later, leaves something to be desired. Mark's play is conceptually brilliant at this score: He sets up two volatile new bingo lanes, and Mark's Y is the most likely of twenty remaining tiles that can go at A12. Once either player plays down to A12, B2–8 may become a viable lane.

6   AALRTWY   PILAW   8K   30   181

Best. Mark scores well and continues to keep lanes open.

7   AARTTXY   TRAY   01   45   226

Great play, splitting the scoring of the Y and X (ATAXY 011 would be a waste), and in the correct order. Not only is the upper right more likely to be blocked; playing at 14F *second* gives Joel one less move to block row 15. Note ARTY would be inferior to TRAY; Mark may need to bingo later from 1H.

8   ?EOOSTX   OX   14E   52   278

At this point, the camera zoomed in to a note Mark had made on his score sheet: `SEXTOOL?' At 15B, this could score 120 pts, but I guess Mark decided it was a phony.

9   ?AEOSST*   ASTOnES*   C1   78   356

Gasps went up from the crowd, who had mainly been considering ASTOnES* at 15A (OSmATES* is 1 extra pt). Then and later, Mark's triple-triple slotting play was widely acclaimed as `brilliant'. While that may be, I can't agree it is the winningest. It offers Joel much better scoring chances, and immediately sacrifices an additional 13 pts, all of which may be critical to Mark winning a close game after his next bingo. OSmATES* 15A still leaves eight bingo lanes open, in particular the top middle TWS horizontally and vertically. In 420 simulations, OSmATES* won 24.5 games (about 6 per cent), pETASOS C1 won 17.5 (4 per cent), and ASTOnES C1 only 8 (2 per cent).

10   ?EEGLIN   LEErING   15D   87   443

Noise in the crowd reached a fever pitch as they saw Mark pick the second blank. Pandemonium ensued as experts tried to predict who would now win. Without knowing Joel's rack, Mark's odds of a win are now 5.5 out of 36: Only if AK, EK, HK, KO, KO or EN (tie) is in the bag. LEErING seems obviously best, but see footnote.

21.5 games, PRANA 36, LIAR (D1) 41, PLAN 44, PIAN 49, and ALAP* 53.

11	AEINOOR	AERIFY	4J	24	460

An agonizing situation for Joel. If KHI 13J were the only out-play, he could block (e.g., OO* M12). But Mark has a second out-play, HONK 5A (also 10 pts). REN* D4 (24) takes a 17–pt lead but leaves (4 x 2) pts on his rack, leading to a 1–pt loss, as does AMORINO 4A. And so, Joel takes a practical approach, with AERIFY: If Mark miscounts and/or does not look for the new HK spot, *Joel* will win by 1 pt!

11	HK	KHI	M2	20	463

Mark does not fall for the trap, and so stays in the match!

Twice Opp Rack (NOO) +6 = 469

Final Joel Wapnick 460

Score Mark Nyman 469

Footnote to Mark's 10th Move: A surprisingly strong alternative is to get efficient points by fishing away just E with MOE* 4B (12), trying for KEeLING or HEeLING on row 15, or GLENLIKE H1 or pENLIGHT 1H (or a smaller TWS bingo sticking Joel with H or K might be enough). Despite Joel's many scoring resources (KRONOR/HOOKER etc. at 2J, KOHL* M5, REIK*?REINK 15E, etc), MOE* 4B garners 8.5 wins out of 72. They are: EK, IK, KE, KH, HK, KR, RK or HE ties (first letter of each pair is the one drawn, and the second letter the one left

in the bag). In short, MOE has an 11.8 per cent winning chance, not much less than LEErING's 15.3 per cent.

Nick concluded his commentary, `Above is quite likely the most miraculous turn-around ever to have been pulled off in an important game – destined to become a classic. I hereby dub it "The Apple Game" (after N.Y., City, the Big Apple).'

Mark had the advantage of starting the final game and led for most of it in spite of some excellent play from his opponent. His winning score to clinch the title was 417 to 369, concluding an epic final against an extremely gracious loser in Joel.

	A	B	C	D	E	F	G	H	I	J	K	L	M	N	O
1	P₃	L₁	A₁	N₁				3W				2L			T₁
2		2W	S₁			3L				3L			K₅	2W	R₁
3			T₁				2L		2L				H₄		A₁
4	2L	M₃	O₁	2W				2L		A₁	E₁	R₁	I₁	F₄	Y₄
5		O₁	N*		2W						2W			O₁	
6		W₄	E₁			3L			3L	J₈			R₁		
7	U₁	N₁	S₁				2L		2L		U₁		2L	M₃	
8	B₃			Q₁₀			Z₁₀	E₁	D₂		P₃	I₁	L₁	A₁	W₄
9	E₁		C₃	U₁	R₁	I₁	O₁		2L		A₁	D₂	2L	B₃	
10	R₁	3L		A₁		D₂	O₁	G₂	E₁	A₁	T₁	E₁		L₁	
11	T₁		F₄	I₁	V₄	E₁	S₁				I₁	N₁		E₁	E₁
12	Y₄	U₁		R₁				2L			T₁				H₄
13		V₄	I₁	S₁	T₁	A₁	E₁	D₂	2L		I₁	2W			I₁
14		A₁			O₁	X₈				3L		C₃		2W	N₁
15	3W			L₁	E₁	E₁	R*	I₁	N₁	G₂		2L			G₂

1994 NATIONAL SCRABBLE CHAMPIONSHIP – FINAL

Mike Willis versus Clive Spate

For the first time the 1994 National Scrabble Championships saw the playoff between the finalists as the best of five games. Mike Willis, NSC champion from ten years earlier, was matched against Clive Spate, the top-rated player of 1994 and a leading figure in the APSP.

Mike had won the first two games. Clive won game three and squeezed to victory in the fourth game by a margin of twelve points. This took the match into its fifth and final game, which we look at here.

Once again Dick Chinnery provides the commentary aided by another top player, Brian Sugar.

Mike Willis

	rack	move	pos	score	total
1	ANNEKRS	ENRANKS	g8a	82	82

Chinnery: Willis has no trouble spotting the bonus playable from this rack. The K lures the bonus to start from 8g but is there a better position for a sacrifice of 8 or 10 points? How about playing ENRANKS at c1a or h1a where any subsequent play onto the S (bonus or otherwise) yields a tws in return. This would be my choice.

Clive Spate

	rack	move	pos	score	total
1	ACEGOZY	AGENCY	k5d	24	24

Chinnery: A useful scoring rack to help counter the bonus deficit. It is always worth checking out the best play retaining the scoring tile (the Z) as well as the best play using that letter. With the Z both ZYGON or GAZON (k4d) score well but the former provides a ready dws Z reply for Willis so I would go for GAZON here, keeping score potential with CEY. Spate goes for the alternative strategy finding a strong turnover play retaining the Z.
Sugar: I quite like the play of COZEN k4d because the Y

2   ENNOPST   PENNON   h3d   9   91

Chinnery: Consultation with OSL reveals a bonus around that A (also spotted by Russell Byers at the live display). Do you know it? Willis doesn't, and settles for a defensive turnover play. A better alternative to reap some points with one less turnover is PONTES m3d for 18, taking out the S and restricting use of the l1d dls/dws position (even more so with the OP-less OSW3!).

Sugar: Willis goes for turnover but this is wrong when good letters are already on the rack! If the bonus is missed then best play is PONY (h10a) keeping the powerful ENTS leave.

3   STEEOSU   ORE   i7d   18   109

Chinnery: Willis doesn't fall for the OUTSEES trap and settles for a few points with attention to rack balance. The U is going to be a bit of a problem though so maybe playing more tiles with TOUSE (d10a), keeping just ES, is strategically better. Similarly TOUSES (m3d).

Sugar: Poor play by Willis. It is normally a cardinal sin to keep duplicate Ss at such an early stage in the game. Best play is ZELS/SUETY.

4   STESUGO   GUYOT   h12a   22   131

Chinnery: GUSTOES was suggested by several players in the audience at the live display but unfortunately this plural is not allowed. GUYOT is neat insofar as it closes off the FOY(S) flexible opening, scores well for low-scoring tiles and leaves a fairly weak letter, the G, at h12. Although some advise using one of the duplicate Ss to increase bonus potential, it can be equally strong strategy to wait until that spare S is the *only* means of bringing a 20–30 point score rather than using it for an extra 2 or 4 points. The other consideration when faced with a duplicate S luxury is that if one is played for a lowly score the opponent immediately guesses you are holding another S. Whether you wish the opponent to know that or not is up to your strategic discretion. TOGUES (b10a) is a neat high- turnover play for a few more points.

Sugar: It remains bad play to continue to hold those two Ss. Playing GUYOTS this turn is better.

5   SESAAOO   COO   k9a   15   146

Sugar: I would suggest a change here, keeping just ES. The turnover and rack leave outweighing the scores on offer.

Chinnery: An awful pickup by Willis and a reaction decision may be to change. But there is probably an equal chance of improving the rack by playing a couple of vowels and of course any points for dumping a few vowels is better than none. It would be nice to play the A and O but the 4 points for AGO h11d does not justify the opening risk. Willis's COO play is a good compromise of score and balance. Opening up the n column for bonuses

leave gives scoring prospects and the AG could combine with an E for COZENAGE for 40 points.

2   OZEFLXY   ZEL   g7d   44   68

Chinnery: Spate has the ideal come-back rack. He is able to continue a two-move strategy, scoring well this turn and retaining powerful scoring options irrespective of pickup.

Sugar: A better play for five points less is FOXY/AY keeping the ZEL move in hand (or FEZ if blocked). This is because of additional turnover and the three letters ZEL offering better bonus potential.

3   OEFXYAI   FOY   j10d   33   101

Chinnery: FOXY and FAIX shout out to be played from 12 but Spate wisely resists the X play this turn in favour of a solid score with F at J10. This takes him practically level and with X options for next turn.

Sugar: Agree with the FOY choice, the leave of AEIX being preferable to OYE.

4   EXAIFMI   FAIX   l2d   37   31

Chinnery: Now is the time for the X to be played whilst scoring places still exist, and giving the lead to Spate for the first time. There appears little to choose between MAXI 13d or FAIX k13a or 12d. On closer inspection though, MAXI leaves an easy-to-use good scoring slot down the m column which can be better restricted with FAIX (12d). FAIX at k13a scores less but offers a possible dws XI opportunity to follow – but would you then play XI and the XI(S) tws risk?

5   EMIALNU   EMU   j4d   24   162

Chinnery: Spate arrives at a bonus rack ... without the bonus! If you know LUMINA then LUMINAE may be tempting but not if you know LUMINA is a plural of LUMEN. Spate should be looking to take a 20-point lead this turn with as much turnover as can be afforded without undue risk. AINE (m2d) scores best for 29 but the MUL leave is weak. I quite fancy LIGNUM h10d for 27 points here, the -UM floaters not being especially risky. Spate opts for a more defensive play with less turnover – EMU (j4d). This restricts the use of E and N of PENNON

SCRABBLE

S
C
R
A
B
B
L
E

should not be a worry, particularly as any play down that column should yield a tws-S opportunity on column o.

6   SESAADI AD   m2d   15   161

Chinnery: With a B there's DIABASES, without a B; nothing! If it helped with the score I would use one of the Ss this turn and look to play 5 tiles, keeping perhaps AS or ES. However, there is a score of 38 using both Ss adjacent to FAIX – can you find it?

Sugar: Willis is too economical with the letters (reminiscing high-score days!). Any play using an S and hooking onto ZEL is better. I would choose DAIS for 20.

7   SESAIJE   JEAN   e5a   22   183

Sugar: With emphasis still on using an S and reaping in some points, a reasonable play here is JEES/ZELS even though this uses both Es.

Chinnery: There is not much with the J here, even considering using an S with it. Willis's JEAN is defensive in removing PENNON floaters whilst keeping a very promising ISES. Willis would be aware that if he gets a bonus it is likely to be playable using the ZEL(S) hook. However, this turn a stronger move is to have a complete clear out and play JASIES (b10a) for 44 and an 18-point lead.

8   SESIBRS   BEGS   l15a   30   213

Chinnery: Willis can take the tws at o8 or the tws at o15. Tile-tracking awareness should conclude the o15 tws is the one to take as, with all the Ss now onboard, the tws at o8 will be available to take next turn. But not vice versa. So Willis plays in the correct position but overlooks the better play of BIGS to keep the E.

Sugar: There are not many Rs played so for a few points less and extra turnover I would opt for BRIGS k15a. If it wasn't for the tws threat at o15, or even nine-timer threat, RIBS (o7d) would be best.

9   SIRSDET   STRIDES   o3d   86   299

Chinnery: Willis was perhaps fortunate to pick that E having played his only E last turn. No question about the play.

10   ABILOT   BOA   d6a   20   319

Sugar: Willis's play would be fine if it wasn't for the awkward duplicate Is on the rack. I would emphasize avoiding rack imbalance at this stage and play either OBIIT (e13a) or GLIB (h12d).

Chinnery: Agree with the need to pay attention to rack leave. BITO (b6a) for 21 points is appealing. Willis knows

for bonus plays and prevents an AX(E) score by Willis. Note MAX(I) now possible.

Sugar: A nice bonus if an R was available is LEMURIAN. I would value turnover greater than defence, and opt for ALUMNI (c13a) for 21, keeping just the E.

6   IALNIW?   WIN   m1a   25   187

Chinnery: Not much dispute about the best play here. Spate's WIN turns out to be unprophetic but everything else is right about it – good score, healthy balance with the blank, retaining the L for COO(L), and taking the tws ahead of the opponent.

7   IAL?GIM   MAILInG   n9d   80   267

Chinnery: No prizes for spotting MAILInG but a few perhaps for knowing the COO(M) hook to play it on to. MAGILP (c3a) is a good alternative if not knowing COOM, but then maybe MAGILP would not be known either. (Its sister-word MEGILP in plural is the anagram of GLIMPSE)!

8   AAEHLRW   WHALE   o5d   x   267

Chinnery: Spate needs to somehow take out the tws at o8 – with Ss and a blank still to come it is a probable high-scoring place for Willis that does not yield a high-scoring reply for Spate. In contrast the ZEL(S) bonus slot will offer a tws reply for Spate. With his strong lead Spate can afford to restrict the tws at o8 with a play such as LAW (m10a). It is unwise to use both the H and W (eg HAW) because the H is useful for a subsequent score (eg HAE m13d). What Spate can't afford to do is lose a turn!

Sugar: A safe play of WAR (m10a) blocks COOM(S). A possible setup play, although a little risky, is WHEEL (f2d) because it takes an A hook and there's only one A and a blank unseen.

9   AAEHLRW   HA   n6d   29   296

Chinnery: The tls at n6 begs use this turn and enables Spate to claw back level and keep a reasonable rack balance. Playing AHA this turn would leave a rack imbalance and unnecessarily use what is now a rare A.

10   AELRWCI   CAGIER   h10d   27   323

Sugar: Spate takes the triple with a healthy turnover but the W should be played first. CLAW b7a for 27 or GREW h12d for 24 are better plays.

Chinnery: Spate would have been aware that the blank is the only remaining goodie (the Q being mixed blessings)

92

that Spate still has that W (from the lost turn) so no need to be too worried about leaving bonus floaters.

| 11 | IILTUUV | change 7 | 0 | 319 |

Chinnery: If five of these tiles could be played keeping a U and one other then that would be favourable to changing. But there are only three- and four-tile plays each leaving unpromising racks, eg VLEI (f14a) for 15 leaving ITUU. The conclusion is to change all seven to go for the blank, or possibly change six and keep a U (depends on your gambling instincts). Interestingly, even this depressing rack can be transformed with an S for UVULITIS!

Sugar: Agree with the change but would consider VIRTU e15a at face value a good defensive alternative, keeping ILU.

| 12 | ENPTTV? | PET | c7a | 22 | 341 |

Sugar: Willis plays PET, presumably aware of (S)PET which he has the blank for. But this is risky because Spate could hit him with QUID or QUIT from a8. Better to play PEEVE f4a or TIP m13a, both plays being out of harms way.

| 13 | NTV?EEU | UVEA | f3d | 7 | 348 |

Unseen letters from Willis' view:

IIIOU HLQRRRTT

Chinnery: Willis lets the U go, no doubt reckoning that the blank will suffice if the Q is picked. His tile tracking would have revealed the likely IR pickup to give a bonus onto (S)PET. UVEA also neatly allows QUEP possibility. This is a very good play by Willis.

Sugar: I would consider VENA e11a, keeping the U, a better play.

| 14 | NT?EEQR | FAT | 12a | 16 | 364 |

Sugar: Willis will know the unseen tiles are IIOU LRRTT so a setup play is tempting, e.g. the b8a for (E)THE. Best play is NTH a8a for 18 which allows QuERN or QuEEN in addition to QUEP. Taking the last two is not a problem given the limited opportunities for Spate's rack.

Chinnery: Willis prefers to leave one in the bag for endgame advantage, encouraged by the fact that he can score 16 points for one tile and also have plays of QuENA and QUEP available for the Q.

| 15 | N?EEQRT | QuENA | d11a | 26 | 390 |

Sugar: Willis can now seal victory with QuENA and several playouts with ERT.

and probably considered the turnover advantageous for that reason.

| 11 | LWDDHIT | LEWD | g14a | 12 | 335 |

Sugar: Strategy here would be to keep that vowel and offload three of four consonants around the E of CAGIER. Spate opts for LEWD but better is DWELT to rid of a T as there are plenty left.

Chinnery: TWIDDLE b14a is a great play to take a timely lead, blocking a number of bonus places. On the down side, it is known that Willis changed seven and, with thirteen tiles unseen it is odds on he has the blank, and that there is rubbish in the bag. The turnover of TWIDDLE is not especially advantageous but the lead it generates is.

| 12 | DHITRUV | DIV | m13a | 14 | 349 |

Unseen letters from Spate's view:

EEIIOU? LNQRRTTV

Chinnery: Spate has to be wary of picking the Q and ensuring he doesn't end up with all consonants on a tight board. His choice of DIV achieves this.

Sugar: I would play VRIL d9a as a defensive measure against Willis's last play, tying the board up nicely. A nice scoring play is DIV (i2d) for 20 points to keep score pressure on Willis.

| 13 | THIURII | PHI | c7d | 9 | 358 |

Sugar: An unfortunate pickup for Spate but his play is wrong. If he has tracked correctly he would notice that it is impossible for Willis to play the Q on the tws at a8 if he has it. Probably wiser to keep the H and settle for MAXI for 13.

Chinnery: PHI cannot be best – it creates two easy bonus slots down from b9 or d9 and Willis is likely to have bonus letters.

| 14 | TURIILO | LI | i2d | 8 | 366 |

Sugar: Spate correctly stops the easy place for the Q which devalues Willis's blank.

Chinnery: LOIR i1d for 13, keeping UIT with a pickup of one tile from EENQRRT? gives a chance of a playout next (QUITE, QUIRT, QUINT) since Willis may have to play the Q in a re-usable position. (Spate must assume Willis has the Q).

| 15 | TURIOR | QUIRT | d11d | 30 | 396 |

Chinnery: Spate knows QUIRT is a losing move because Willis can play out next. A possible last ditch attempt could be to play OR (e10a) to block all obvious existing playouts and hope that the surprise element of the move may force an error. Although this leaves TRIE and creates two playouts with OuTER or ROuTE that blank U could be confusing. Assuming Willis doesn't spot these then he cannot block Spate's QUIRT playout and needs to realize that he can win by one point by playing ETH or REH a8a.

16	TRE	RITE	c13a	8	398	16	OR left

Willis +2	400
Spate -2	394

	A	B	C	D	E	F	G	H	I	J	K	L	M	N	O
1	3W			2L				3W				2L	W_4	I_1	N_1
2		2W				3L		L_1		3L		F_4	A_1	T_1	
3			2W			U_1	2L	P_3	I_1			A_1	D_2		S_1
4	2L			2W		V_4		E_1		E_1		I_1			T_1
5				J_8	E_1	A_1	N_1			M_3	A_1	X_8			R_1
6		3L		B_3	O_1	A_1		N_1		U_1	G_2			H_4	I_1
7			P_3	E_1	T_1		Z_{10}	O_1	O_1		E_1		2L	A_1	D_2
8	3W		H_4	2L		E_1	N_1	R_1	A_1	N_1	K_5	S_1			E_1
9			I_1			L_1		E_1		C_3	O_1	O_1	M_3		S_1
10		3L				3L		C_3		F_4	Y_4		A_1		
11			Q_{10}	U^*	E_1	N_1	A_1			O_1	2W		I_1		
12	2L		U_1				G_2	U_1	Y_4	O_1	T_1		L_1		2L
13			R_1	I_1	T_1	E_1	2L	I_1	2L			D_2	I_1	V_4
14		2W		R_1		3L	L_1	E_1	W_4	D_2			N^*	
15	3W			T_1				R_1			B_3	E_1	G_2	S_1

SCRABBLE® CHALLENGES

Now that you've heard and seen how experienced players put their ideas into practice, it's your turn to take on the challenge presented by a series of familiar Scrabble situations.

The bonus of 50 points awarded for playing all seven tiles on your rack in one turn is the secret of high Scrabble scores. Spotting seven-letter words from an apparent jumble of letters takes practice and that's what the first four types of challenge featured here provide.

It's obviously quite impossible to try the more than 5,000 ways of arranging your seven letters (assuming none of the tiles are blanks). Experienced players develop ways of spotting likely combinations to help them quickly focus on possible words. You might begin by looking for familiar groups of letters: -ATE,

DIS-, -ED, -ER, EST, -GHT and so on through the alphabet. Then there are letters that often go together in pairs, such as BL-, CR-, DR-, FL-, GR-, -MM-, -NN-, SP-, TH- and WH-.

Certain letters seldom come together and it's worth knowing all the unlikely combinations like DP, FK, HR and SG.

Another useful way of forming seven-letter words is to try making a three-letter word and a four-letter word from the tiles on your rack. In this way you won't overlook any seven-letter words like DOGTROT, RUNLETS and SIRLOIN.

Several different approaches to forming seven-letter words are tackled here. All the answers are at the back, including alternative solutions in those cases where there is more than one possible answer.

CONSONANT PLAY

Look at the sets of three consonants given below. Can you find the seven-letter word which begins with the first letter and contains the other two in the order given?

1 V C X	16 P V H
2 H W V	17 T Z Q
3 J C Z	18 J W K
4 F M X	19 P Y Z
5 W P W	20 V H C
6 D W V	21 B X F
7 Q Z Y	22 N W K
8 V D K	23 L C J
9 X P H	24 G T X
10 Y H M	25 H T Z
11 M W F	26 L B P
12 K L J	27 F B X
13 F Y V	28 W W X
14 D W W	29 J K W
15 N H W	30 W K H
	31 B Z Q
	32 C M Q
	33 P K X
	34 J Z M
	35 S X D
	36 W X K
	37 C D Z
	38 M J Y
	39 B X W
	40 D J Y

THE TWO-BLANK CHALLENGE

A rack containing two blanks should be well on the way to making a seven-letter word. But it's not always so easy. Sometimes, as if as a punishment for our being given two blanks, the other letters seem determined to cause us difficulties.

All the combinations given below, with two blanks, make at least one seven-letter word. In most cases, they are not too obscure, even if some of them are not exactly everyday words. Can you find the elusive bonuses? The number of possible answers is given.

ONE ANSWER

1   QXEIU
2   ZSBWH
3   YYRHM
4   CFKRY
5   THWYT
6   JIDIT
7   GHKTU
8   AVDVD
9   EFIIO
10 HIHOW
11 WHOOK
12 GHMMO
13 CFKRN
14 SSSSA
15 XWIBT
16 CFLMR
17 GOBAZ
18 MNNYY
19 CCOOZ
20 MAVAC
21 LLLFY
22 XYHLT
23 AAAJP

24 SWGYY
25 CKLNT
26 SMPHV
27 QUOOY
28 CUWNR
29 DHMUX
30 BBCOW
31 BBZIT
32 JKYLL
33 FGIUU
34 PJUMO
35 HGYMP

TWO ANSWERS

1   LMUUU
2   EEEER
3   XLPPE
4   YEYOD
5   FLOWW
6   FLWHT
7. LBCIL
8   AAUUS
9   SYSOJ
10 ITQUV
11 ODODO
12 AAGOZ
13 ZIHUA
14 HOTMT

THREE ANSWERS

1   COOVA
2   PYXHA
3   KGHRE
4   FEWTH

FOUR ANSWERS

1   OOOZY
2   GHRTW
3   AEIOU

97

ANAGRAMS

Find the seven-letter word from each combination below. All except 2–10 make one word only.

ONE TO TEN

Number one has one valid answer, number two has two, and so on up to number ten which has ten valid answers.

1 TRUEMIX
2 VEWHERO
3 INRODES
4 SCREEDE
5 RANDELS
6 ITSDOPE
7 ITLEANS
8 REPSITS
9 RAINGES
10 GINTEAS

TEN WITH A

All the answers begin with A.

11 YOURARM
12 MACALAN
13 FAYLING
14 LAXLOOT
15 SUREBOA
16 ISACOAL
17 ACHERRY
18 REALLOG
19 HEAVICE
20 YOOFALL

GETTING AROUND

Ten modes of transport. How far can you get with them?

21 LEBICCY
22 CORTOES
23 IMBOSUN
24 PINABLE
25 KATZRIB
26 RELYLOT
27 TATACOB
28 DOBBLES
29 CRAMRAT
30 JILTFOE

THE NEWCOMERS

All the answers first appeared in the 1994 edition of OSW, so think of words you have probably started hearing in the last few years.

31 WADEFAT
32 RUTLOLO
33 FSFACED
34 OAKRAKE
35 SAMBBUG
36 MODISOF
37 SPAYKED
38 DARKYOW
39 ZEMISSI
40 ROSEKIP

THE TOUGH TEN

Ten difficult ones – find half of these and you're on the way to being an expert.

41 SEADELL
42 LEAVENM
43 TYDFLOW
44 SOMBOLE
45 INYYPEG
46 PAYEXIT
47 RAGFERN
48 TRICOCE
49 USPRAWL
50 ELKWEEP

TEN WITH Z

To finish with, ten combinations containing a Z.

51 NEENIBZ
52 DOZIEDI
53 POZYTOE
54 LADSRIZ
55 HERZEST
56 LUBREEZ
57 GETZTEA
58 HABITEZ
59 FEZLUST
60 UZEEXIT

S
C
R
A
B
B
L
E

OUT IN TWO MOVES

In a close finish, the player who can play out his or her final rack in two moves can often pinch the game. See if you can split each rack below into two valid words, which could give you that `out in two moves' and a win.

1 WUVUSOM
2 AAANIII
3 ZUPDOPH
4 AACKIOU
5 NYGTWNY
6 IOULLLL
7 ZUJISOQ
8 MOCDOWD
9 UOGNUOY
10 AAAATHH
11 QUCPSYA
12 AEHWOOO
13 IIUUPPT
14 AJKXYZE
15 AJKXYZO
16 IIIALCV
17 MYPENGN
18 APIGVYZ
19 HIVCRLY
20 TPEUEUE
21 AJEAKOY
22 BREEIIA
23 HHYYCMT
24 EIMECYE
25 GULIOVU
26 HUVCACA
27 BARRYGR
28 HEVINTV
29 LLIIOOO
30 YIVAUEF
31 YVYVINA
32 AEIOOXZ
33 BIXLVEY
34 AIOUHYY
35 BXEBEST
36 IIIFFEW
37 CVFKALE
38 BPETVWY
39 FAKTBAJ
40 PRIBSYV

BACKWORDS

Your task here is to find as many words as you can of six letters or more, ending in the three letters given. The number after each set of letters is a target for you to aim at – but you may find more.

1 STO 5
2 IEL 6
3 AWK 4
4 LEX 8
5 FEW 3
6 TIM 5
7 BUS 12
8 TAX 4
9 HAM 6
10 ICH 8
11 LAN 8
12 DOX 3
13 HAW 10
14 LOO 5
15 SEA 3
16 NZE 4
17 BOO 5
18 CAP 8
19 JAW 3
20 BAR 6
21 DUS 4
22 DAM 6
23 ERO 6
24 ATO 8
25 TOM 6
26 ARM 8
27 OUD 8
28 NNA 8
29 OMB 8
30 TTO 12

31 OWL 5
32 NZA 6
33 PIN 12
34 RIM 6
35 HOL 6
36 FIX 5
37 UIN 8
38 RTO 4
39 FLY 15
40 BIN 6
41 LIX 4
42 HON 8
43 IGO 5
44 BUG 6
45 KEL 4

46 TOO 3
47 GUN 6
48 CUP 5
49 SAW 6
50 GAM 6
51 BOW 5
52 ASK 4
53 EXT 6
54 CAR 6
55 IAD 5
56 ROO 8
57 BAG 8
58 HEW 5
59 JET 4
60 SAY 6

SCRABBLE PUZZLES

There are twenty Scrabble puzzles here to help you improve your play. Each puzzle shows the board at a certain stage in a game and the seven tiles that one player has at that stage. Your aim (except in the last two, which are slightly different) is to make the highest possible score by adding one or more letters on the rack to those on the board to form a new word or words, just as you would in a real game.

Although there are some fairly outlandish words shown on the boards, you won't need to know any obscure words to find the highest score. You may, however, need to consult the list of two- and three-letter words.

In these puzzles the two blank tiles are represented by '?' on the rack. Once played, they are denoted as an '*' against the letter designated.

PUZZLE 1

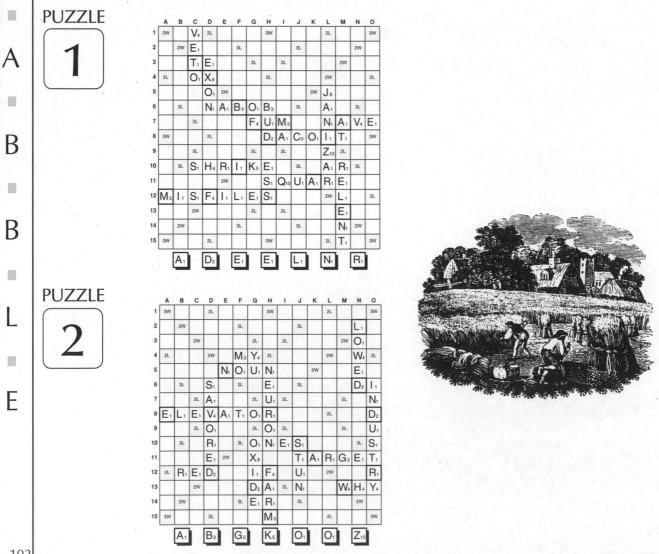

Rack: A₁ D₂ E₁ E₁ L₁ N₁ R₁

PUZZLE 2

Rack: A₁ B₃ G₂ K₅ O₁ O₁ Z₁₀

S
C
R
A
B
B
L
E

Puzzle 3 rack: J₈ Y₄ M₃ A₁ T₁ E₁ S₁

Puzzle 4 rack: A₁ C₃ E₁ R₁ S₁ T₁ ?₀

Puzzle 5 rack: A₁ E₁ N₁ N₁ S₁ T₁ T₁

S C R A B B L E

PUZZLE 6

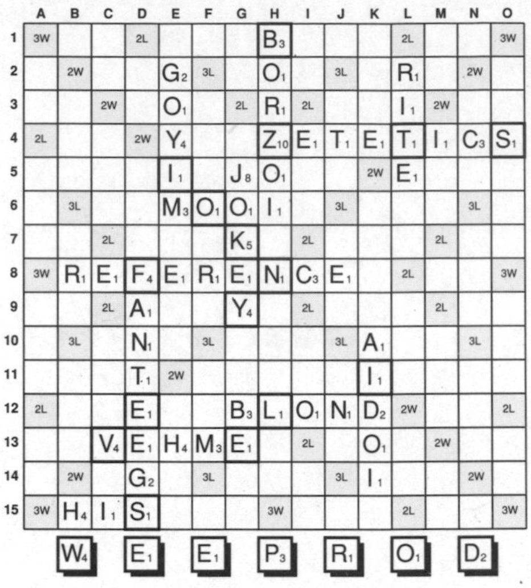

PUZZLE 7

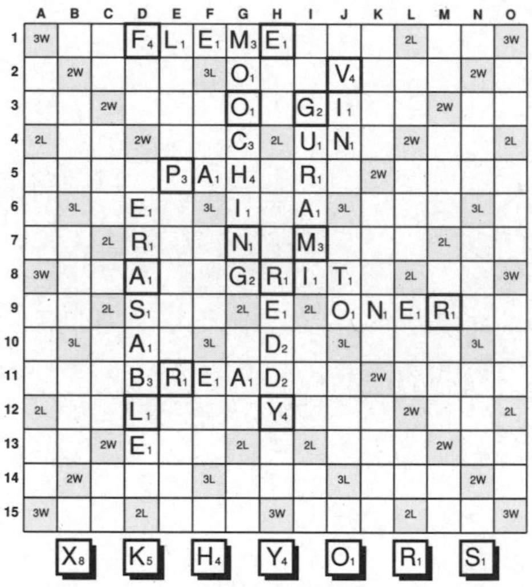

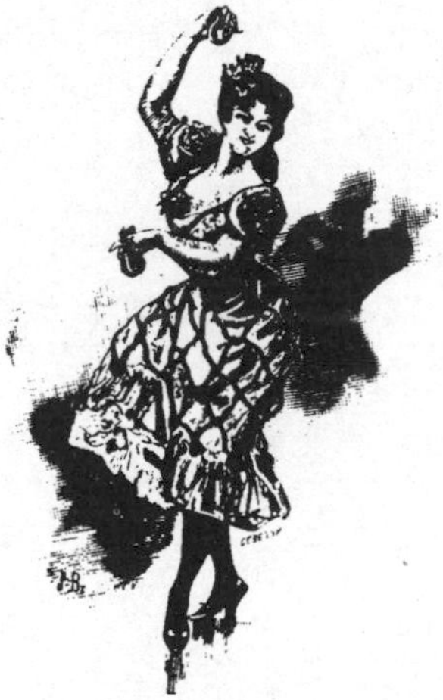

PUZZLE 8

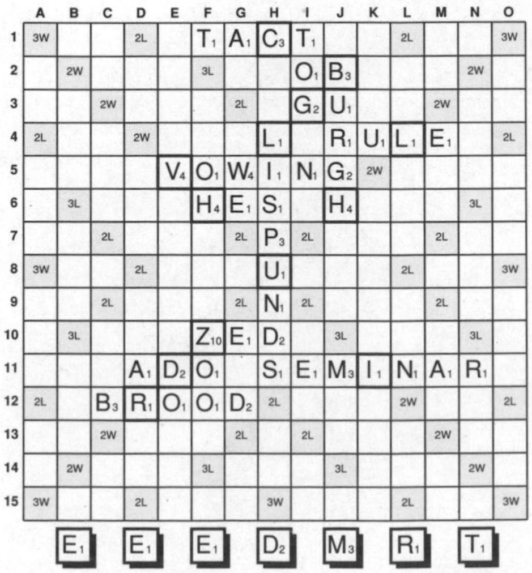

PUZZLE 9

	A	B	C	D	E	F	G	H	I	J	K	L	M	N	O
1	3W			2L				3W				F4	I1	Z10	3W
2		P3	R1	O1	V4	E1				C3	R1	A1	N1	2W	
3		U1	2W			M3	A1	T1	C3	H4			2W		
4	2L	L1		2W				U1				2W			2L
5		K5			2W	A1	G2	R1	E1	E1	2W				
6		H4				3L		B3		3L				3L	
7		A1	2L				J8	O1	W4				2L		
8	3W			2L			A1	T1	E1		O1	I1			3W
9			2L				R1		Y4	O1	N1		2L		
10		3L			B3	3L	F4			V4				3L	
11					E1	M3	U1			A1	2W				
12	2L			2W	G2	E1	L1	2L		L1	E1	A1			2L
13			2W	I1	O1		2L		2L				2W		
14		2W		O1		3L				3L				2W	
15	3W			2L				3W				2L			3W

A1 E1 L1 R1 S1 X8 ?0

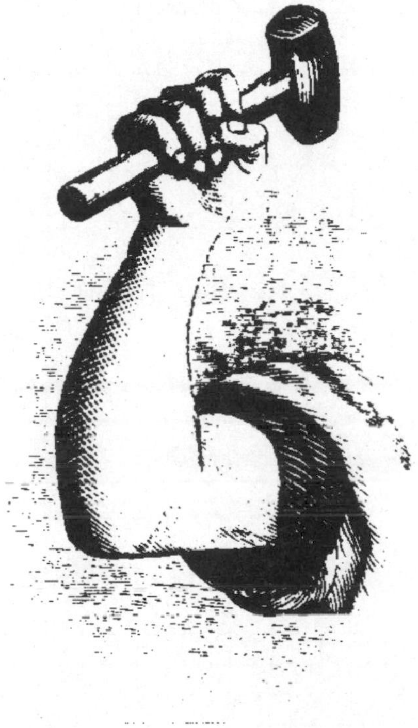

PUZZLE 10

	A	B	C	D	E	F	G	H	I	J	K	L	M	N	O
1	3W			2L				3W	Q10	U1	I1	V4	E1	R1	3W
2		2W				3L				N1				2W	
3			2W				2L		2L	D2			2W		
4	2L			2W				2L		O1	D2	2W			2L
5					2W						R1				
6		M3	A1	N1	I1	C3				F4	A1			3L	
7	N1	O1	W4			A1	2L		L1	A1	G2		J8	O1	
8	O1	D2	A1	2L	O1	K5	A1	P3	I1		S1	H4	E1		3W
9			2L			E1	2L		M3				T1	A1	X8
10		W4	I1	T1	H4	Y4			B3	O1				3L	
11					2W					O1	2W				
12	2L			2W				Z10		B3		2W			2L
13			2W				P3	A1	C3	I1	F4	Y4	2W		
14		2W				3L		G2		T1	A1	E1	L1	2W	
15	3W			2L				3W				2L			3W

D2 E1 E1 N1 R1 S1 S1

PUZZLE 11

	A	B	C	D	E	F	G	H	I	J	K	L	M	N	O
1	3W			2L				3W				2L			3W
2		2W				3L				3L				2W	
3			2W				2L		2L				2W		
4	2L			2W				2L				2W			2L
5					2W						2W			E1	A1
6		3L				3L				3L				X8	I1
7			2L				B3		M3	U1	F4	T1	I1		R1
8	3W			F4	L1	U1	R1	R1	Y4			2L	D2	A1	W4
9			2L				A1		2L				2L		A1
10		3L				3L	C3			3L				3L	V4
11					2W		K5				2W				E1
12	Q10	U1	I1	N1	T1	E1	S1	2L				2W			2L
13			2W				2L		2L				2W		
14		2W				3L				3L				2W	
15	3W			2L				3W				2L			3W

A1 E1 I1 L1 N1 S1 T1

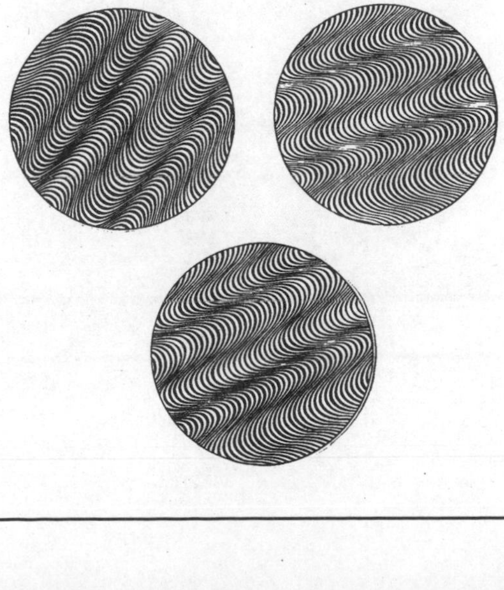

S C R A B B L E

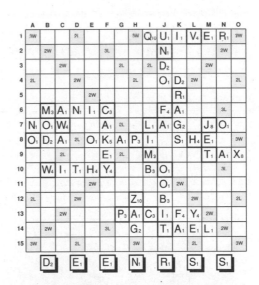

S C R A B B L E

PUZZLE

12

	A	B	C	D	E	F	G	H	I	J	K	L	M	N	O
1	3W			2L				3W				2L			3W
2		2W				3L		R_1		3L	T_1			2W	
3			2W				2L	E_1	2L	M_3	A_1	G_2	I_1		
4	2L			2W				V_4			N_1	2W			2L
5	B_3	L_1	A_1	I_1	Z_{10}	E_1		I_1			T_1				
6		3L				R_1	E_1	S_1	T_1	R_1	A_1	I_1	N_1	3L	
7			2L				2L	E_1	2L		L_1		2L		
8	3W			2L				D_2		H_4	U_1	L_1	L_1		3W
9			2L				2L		2L	O_1	S_1		2L		
10		3L				3L				P_3				3L	
11					2W						2W				
12	2L			2W				2L				2W			2L
13			2W				2L		2L				2W		
14		2W				3L				3L				2W	
15	3W			2L				3W				2L			3W

A_1 C_3 I_1 N_1 O_1 T_1 $?_0$

PUZZLE

13

	A	B	C	D	E	F	G	H	I	J	K	L	M	N	O
1	3W			2L				3W				2L			3W
2		2W				3L				3L				2W	
3			2W				2L		2L				2W		
4	2L			2W				2L				2W			2L
5					2W						2W				
6		3L				3L				3L				3L	
7			2L				2L		2L				2L		
8	3W			2L				Q_{10}	U_1	I_1	Z_{10}	Z*	I_1	F_4	Y_4
9			2L				2L		2L				2L		
10		3L				3L				3L				3L	
11					2W						2W				
12	2L			2W				2L				2W			2L
13			2W				2L		2L				2W		
14		2W				3L				3L				2W	
15	3W			2L				3W				2L			3W

A_1 B_3 E_1 I_1 N_1 R_1 U_1

PUZZLE

14

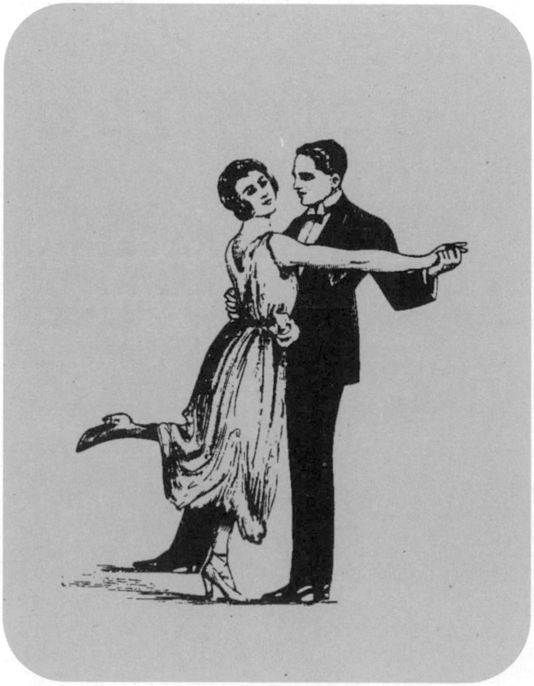

	A	B	C	D	E	F	G	H	I	J	K	L	M	N	O
1	3W			2L				3W				2L			3W
2		2W				3L				3L				2W	
3			2W				2L		2L				2W		
4	2L			2W				2L				2W			2L
5					2W						M_3				
6		3L				M_3				3L	A_1			3L	
7			2L			A_1	2L	F_4	2L		N_1		2L		
8	3W			2L	I_1	N_1	Q_{10}	U_1	I_1	R_1	Y_4	2L			3W
9			P_3			E_1	2L	B_3	2L				2L		
10		B_3	A_1	T_1	C_3	H_4				3L				3L	
11			R_1		2W						2W				
12	2L		T_1	2W			D_2	J_8	I_1	N_1	N_1	I_1			2L
13		K_5	Y_4	A_1	N_1	I_1	Z_{10}	E_1	D_2				2W		
14		2W				F_4	O_1	E_1		3L				2W	
15	3W			2L				3W				2L			3W

P_3 R_1 A_1 T_1 E_1 S_1 I_1

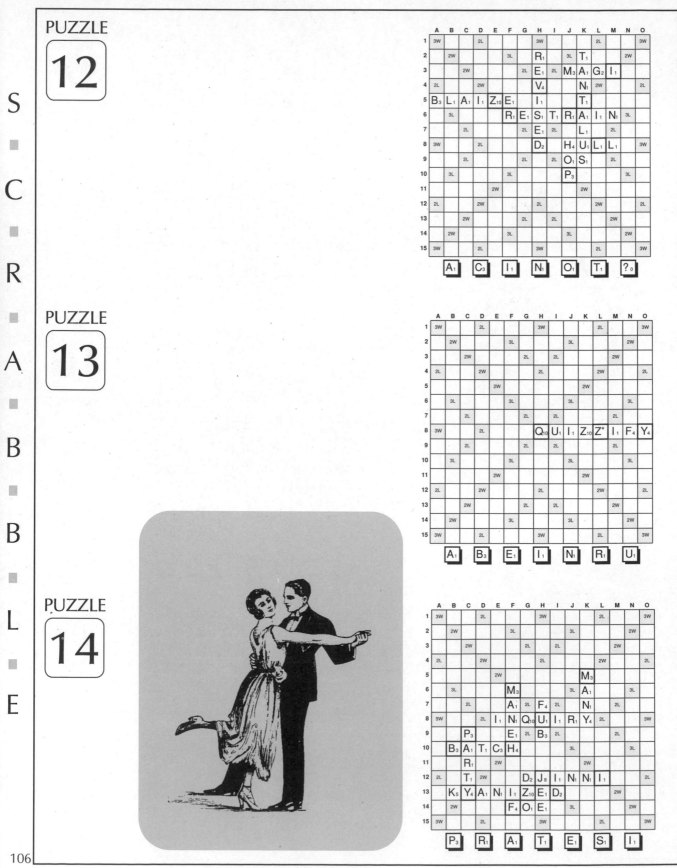

PUZZLE 15

	A	B	C	D	E	F	G	H	I	J	K	L	M	N	O
1	3W			F_4				3W			B_3	2L	T_1		3W
2		2W		R_1	A_1	J_8				3L	U_1		O_1	2W	
3			2W	A_1		O_1	X_8	I_1	D_2	I_{10}	Z_{10}	E_1	R_1		
4	2L			Y_4					2L		$Z*$	2W	U_1		2L
5				S_1	2W						2W		L_1		
6		3L				3L			3L				O_1	3L	
7			2L			2L		2L					S_1		
8	3W		2L			2L		S_1	O_1	L_1	D_2	I_1	E_1	R_1	3W
9		2L					.	A_1	2L			2L			
10	3L				3L			V_4				3L			
11			2W		S_1	L_1	A_1	K_5	E_1	D_2					
12	2L		2W					G_2				2W			2L
13		2W					2L	E_1	2L				2W	.	
14		2W				3L		R_1		3L				2W	
15	3W		2L					3W			2L				3W

Rack: A_1 C_3 C_3 H_4 R_1 T_1 Y_4

PUZZLE 16

	A	B	C	D	E	F	G	H	I	J	K	L	M	N	O
1	3W			2L				3W				2L			3W
2		2W				3L				3L				2W	
3			2W				2L		2L			2W			
4	2L			2W				C_3				2W			2L
5					2W			R_1		2W					
6		3L				3L		A_1		3L			3L		
7			2L			2L		M_3	2L				2L		
8	G_2	O_1	T_1	2L			O_1	B_3			2L				3W
9		O_1					W_4	O_1	U_1	L_1	D_2	S_1	T_1		
10		3L	R_1	A_1	Z_{10}	E_1	E_1	M_3	3L				3L		
11				2W				B_3		2W					
12	2L			2W			2L	O_1			2W				2L
13		2W					2L	N_1				2W			
14		2W				3L		E_1	3L			.	2W		
15	3W			2L				S_1			2L				3W

Rack: R_1 E_1 T_1 A_1 I_1 N_1 A_1

PUZZLE 17

	A	B	C	D	E	F	G	H	I	J	K	L	M	N	O
1	3W			2L			3W				2L				3W
2		2W				3L				3L			2W		
3			2W			2L		2L			2W				
4	2L			2W				2L				2W			2L
5					2W	E₁		L	A₁	D₂					
6		3L	C₃	O₁	R₁	N₁	E₁	A₁	L	3L			3L		
7			2L			J₈		M₃				2L			
8	3W		H₄	A₁	B₃	O₁	O₁	B₃			2L			3W	
9			2L			Y₄		2L				2L			
10		3L	R₁	E₁	D₂	I₁	I₁	D₂		3L			3L		
11			A₁	2W		N₁			2W						
12	2L		P₃			G₂	2L				2W			2L	
13	O₁	P₃	I₁	N₁	G₂	2L		2L				2W			
14		2W		E₁		3L				3L			2W		
15	3W			R₁			3W				2L				3W

A₁ E₁ G₂ I₁ R₁ V₄ Y₄

PUZZLE 18

	A	B	C	D	E	F	G	H	I	J	K	L	M	N	O
1	3W			2L			3W				2L				3W
2		2W				3L				3L			2W		
3			2W			2L		2L			2W				
4	2L			2W				2L				2W			2L
5					2W					2W					
6		3L		F₄	A₁	M₃	E₁		3L				3L		
7			2L		I₁	B₃	I₁	S₁				2L			
8	3W			2L	B₃	U₁	N₁	K₅			2L			3W	
9			2L		S₁	T₁	A₁	Y₄				2L			
10		3L				3L				3L			3L		
11					2W					2W					
12	2L			2W				2L				2W			2L
13			2W			2L		2L			2W				
14		2W				3L				3L			2W		
15	3W			2L			3W				2L				3W

A₁ E₁ L₁ L₁ R₁ T₁ Y₄

In these last two puzzles, rather than necessarily finding the top score, you are asked to find the move which is most likely to bring you a win. You should note that it is close to the end of the game, and once you have placed the tiles on the board as shown, and filled your own rack, you will know, or be close to knowing, what tiles your opponent is holding.

PUZZLE 19

You are 7 points behind with the board and rack as shown, and you have to play. How can you guarantee a win?

A	B	C	D	E	F	G	H	I	J	K	L	M	N	O
A_1			2L				G_2			2L				3W
C_3	O_1	W_4	D_2	3L			O_1	Y_4		3L			2W	
E_1		E_1	Q_{10}	U_1	I_1	P_3	S_1			2L		2W		
2L			U_1	N_1		2L	G_2	I_1	T_1	E_1				2L
	L_1	I_1	G^*	R_1	O_1	I_1	N_1			2W				
	3L		P_3		3L		A_1	H_4				3L		
		2L	L_1			H_4	A_1	T_1	I_1	N_1	G_2	2L		F_4
3W			W_4	O_1	X_8	E_1	N_1			U_1	V_4	E_1	A_1	
		3L	R_1				M_3	I_1	N_1	D_2		2L		
	3L		E_1	R_1	E_1				3L				3L	
			A_1	Y_4	U_1			F_4		2W				
2L		2W	K_5				J_8	O_1	R_1	A_1	M_3			C_3
	B_3	L_1	A_1	S_1	T_1	E_1	R_1			E_1	O_1	N_1		I_1
2W				3L	A_1			3L				2W	D_2	
3W		2L					T_1	R_1	I_1	Z_{10}	O_1	N^*	E_1	S_1

Rack: A_1 D_2 E_1 I_1 O_1 T_1 V_4

PUZZLE 20

You are 20 points ahead, with the board and rack as shown, and you are to play. What should you play to maximize your chance of winning?

A	B	C	D	E	F	G	H	I	J	K	L	M	N	O
3W	V_4		E_1	S^*	T_1	E_1	R_1	I_1	F_4	Y_4	2L			3W
	E_1	W_4	E_1	3L				A_1					2W	S_1
	G_2	O_1			V_4	A_1	L_1	I_1	N_1	E_1	S_1	2W		O_1
2L		U_1	2W		I_1		2L		D_2		O_1			L_1
M_3	I_1	N_1	X_8	2W	L_1				O_1	2W	U_1	R_1		I_1
O_1	3L	D_2			L_1				M_3		K_5	A_1	E_1	D_2
Z_{10}	O_1	2L			I_1		2L	Q_{10}	I_1	S_1		D_2	A_1	E_1
E_1	E_1		2L				U_1	N_1			2L			R_1
		2L				T_1	I_1	N_1			2L			
	3L		J_8	A_1	B_3		N_1		3L			3L		
			W_4	A_1	F_4	T_1			2W					
2L			2W		T_1	A_1	E_1			2W				2L
	2W				C_3	2L		2L			2W			
2W		P_3	U_1	G_2	H_4				3L			2W		
3W	C_3	R_1	O_1	P_3			3W			2L				3W

Rack: A_1 E_1 G_2 H_4 R_1 S_1 T_1

SCRABBLE® QUIZ

This quiz contains 100 assorted questions to test your word power and Scrabble skills.

1 What letter does the blank represent on the board below?

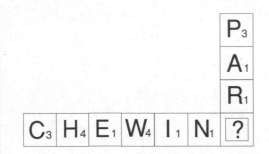

2 Which one of the following is not an allowable word?

SEEABLE, HEARABLE, TASTABLE, TOUCHABLE.

3 Can you find at least six common six-letter words which contain 3 As?

4 You may not know these words, but they all have a much commoner anagram. Can you find them?

BROUZES, MUTAGEN, NUCULES.

5 Place two letters after HYDROS to make an eight-letter word.

6 How many words of three letters or more can you get from the letters ABCDE? You may not use any letter more than once in the same word.

7 Which one of the following is not an allowable word?

WALES, FRANCE, SPAIN, RUSSIA.

8 Compound words can be among the hardest to spot, such as re-arranging ANYALLDD to find your LANDLADY. Can you find the compound words here?

HELLYFEW, REENEILY, FOOTPITH, TESCOPOD.

9 Two of the following words are allowed and two are not. Can you sort them out?

UNCLIMBED, UNSCALED, UNTOPPED, UNMOUNTED.

10 Can you spot the nine-timer on the board below? Your rack is DEDEPOW.

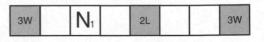

11 Sometimes you can remember seven-letter words by learning which letters combine with a six-letter combination you will recognize, such as your name or part of your address. How many seven-letter words can you find using these six-letter combinations plus a blank?

ANDREW, CAROLE, PALMER, DUNDEE.

12 What letter does the blank represent on the board below?

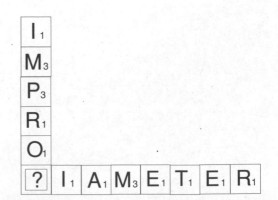

13 Place two letters after DEADLINE to make a ten-letter word.

14 Only one of the following is an allowable word. Which one?

RENTINGS, RIPPINGS, SHREDDINGS, TEARINGS,

15 Can you solve these anagrams? Warning: they all start with a very unlikely pair of letters, e.g. ROBIRS would make the word SBIRRO. (A sbirro is an Italian policeman.)

HARSDAD, PEGFINN, GRIDMAN, MULVE.

16 Find at least six common five-letter words containing two Vs.

17 How many words of three letters or more can you get from the letters FGHIJ? You may not use any letter more than once in the same word.

18 What is five sevenths of sixteen?

19 Many exclamations are allowable words, such as LO and ALAS. Sometimes you can even make a bonus from one. Unscramble these anagrams to find two exclamations of encouragement, and one of disapproval.

PAYSAUDI, TAYBOAT, TCHARGE.

20 What letter does the blank represent on the board below?

21 Which one of the following is not an allowable word?

FRENCH, FLEMISH, DUTCH, DANISH.

22 Find five anagrams of TREELAD – all common words.

23 Can you spot the nine-timer on the board below. Your rack is IIIAURD.

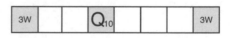

24 Can you find an appropriate anagram of BRING UP?

25 And how about an anagram of BEDROOM – appropriate for some, less so for others.

26 Two of the following words are allowed and two are not. Which are which?

ASSISTEE, MURDEREE, RECEIVEE, VISITEE.

27 Place two letters after NOODLED to make a nine-letter word.

28 Which one of the following can be lengthened by adding one letter to the end of it, and what letter is it?

CRIED, MOANED, MOPED, SKULKED.

29 How many words of three letters or more can you get from the letters KLMNO? You may not use any letter more than once in the same word.

30 The letters RETAIN form the most powerful six-letter combination for making seven-letter words. RETAIN plus a blank makes over fifty bonus words. Can you think of at least twenty?

31 What letter does the blank represent on the board below?

						F$_4$
						L$_1$
						A$_1$
						M$_3$
						I$_1$
						N$_1$
						G$_2$
S$_1$	T$_1$	A$_1$	M$_3$	P$_3$	E$_1$	D$_2$	?

32 Which one of the following is not an allowable word?

   NIGER, MALI, GABON, ZAIRE.

33 How many seven-letter words can you find using these six-letter combinations plus a blank?

   SANDRA, EDWARD, DAVIES, DORSET.

34 Can you find at least five common five-letter words containing four vowels?

35 Which one of these is not an allowable word?

   DICKENS, SHAW, WILDE, GILBERT.

36 And talking of writers, find two seven-letter words from T S ELIOT. One is certainly an everyday word, the other is not inconsiderably less common.

37 Can you find the nine-timer on the board below? Your rack is RETAIN and a blank.

| 3W | S$_1$ | | 2L | | | 3W |

114

38 Which one of the following is not an allowable word?

WELSH, GERMAN, POLISH, RUSSIAN.

39 What letter does the blank represent on the board below?

| T₁ | H₄ | A₁ | T₁ | C₃ | H₄ | ? |

A₁
D₂
V₄
A₁
N₁
C₃
E₁

40 Which one of the following is not an allowable word?

DOURLY, GRIMLY, SOURLY, SULLENLY.

41 How many words of three letters or more can you get from the letters PQRSTU? You may not use any letter more than once in the same word.

42 Place two letters after MARROWS to make a nine-letter word.

43 Can you find the compound words in these four anagrams?

HITAGRIT, THYFOAL, DONAMWAM, REFUGIN.

44 Which one of the following is not an allowable word?

CYPRUS, MOROCCO, MALTA, JORDAN.

45 Find at least four common six-letter words containing three or more Os.

46 What letter does the blank represent on the board below?

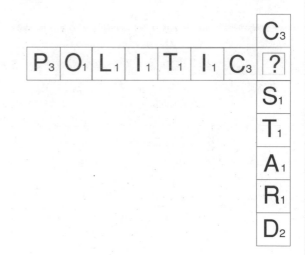

C₃

| P₃ | O₁ | L₁ | I₁ | T₁ | I₁ | C₃ | ? |

S₁
T₁
A₁
R₁
D₂

47 Can you find anagrams for the following words? Anyone between young adult and middle-aged should find them.

TENTWISE, SHITTIER, FOISTER, IFFIEST.

48 Which two letters follow GAZE to make a six-letter word (apart from the obvious GAZERS)?

49 Two of the following are allowed and two are not. Can you sort them out?

RESOLE, REHEEL, RESHOE, REBOOT.

50 Can you spot the nine-timer on the board below? Your rack is GHNRSTT.

51 Which one of the following is not an allowable word?

CHINESE, JAPANESE, SIAMESE, AFGHAN.

52 And which one of these is no good?

CHILE, PERU, CANADA, JAPAN.

53 Neither SCOTLAND nor ENGLAND is an allowable word, but both have a valid anagram. Any ideas?

54 To complete our world tour, IRELAND looks a good combination but it does not have a valid anagram. However, it combines with six other letters to make eight-letter words. How many can you find?

55 How many words of three letters or more can you get from the letters VWXYZ? For this one, you may use the same letter more than once in the same word.

56 Which one of the following is not an allowable word?

DOGGISH, CATTISH, SNAKISH, WORMISH.

57 Can you find a valid anagram of REAL SON?

58 What letter does the blank represent on the board below?

59 What two letters follow ZEBRA to make a seven-letter word?

60 There is a sprinkling of words starting with X, apart from XI, XU and XYLOPHONE.

Match the X-words below to their correct meanings in the right-hand column.

XEBEC — A covered portico.

XYSTER — Very dry hair.

XYSTUS — Yellow.

XANTHIC — A three-masted boat..

XERASIA — Designs on wood made with a hot poker.

XYLOPYROGRAPHY — A surgical implement.

61 What connects the words IT, INCITE and OOLOGY?

62 Can you match these Q words to their correct meanings?

QUAGGA — A Central American bird.

QUANT — A mnemonic of knotted cords.

QUASSIA — An extinct South African ass.

QUETZAL — A humorous medley of tunes.

QUIPU — A South American tree.

QUODLIBET — A pole for punting.

63 Some more words which start with unusual pairs of letters, like SBIRRO. Can you sort them out?

MOSKJABS, CENTE, ALOVEGAS, IMRUTTY.

64 Can you spot the nine-timer on the board below? Your rack is ADEOOTT.

65 A CARFAX is (a) a fax machine in a car (b) a type of fish (c) a machine for digging (d) a crossroads?

66 A CARLOCK is (a) a lock on a car (b) a porcelain ornament (c) a type of gelatine (d) a witch.

67 A CARPORT IS (a) a parking-place for a car (b) a fishing hook (c) a dish of mixed fruit (d) an instrument for drawing straight lines on a sphere?

68 What is the Scrabble significance of 8, 12, 17, 24, 164?

69 The middle word in the middle column of the middle page of OSW (3rd Edition) is (a) LOLLY-GAGGING (b) MANTEEL (c) NET?

70 UNLIVES is defined in *Chambers* as `lives in the contrary manner; lives down; deprives of life.' How is UNDIES defined?

71 Starting with the nine-letter word as shown, remove one letter at a time and shuffle the letters to obtain an eight-letter word, then a seven, and so on down to two. Some letters are already filled in to give you a start. There is more than one answer to this.

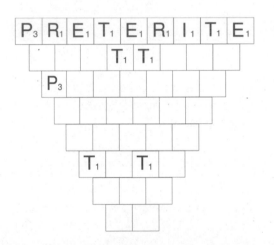

72 Your rack is ELOOPRS. There are lots of bonus possibilities worth considering: LOOPERS, POOLERS, SLOOPER, SPOOLER, RELOOPS, REPOOLS, RESLOOP, RESPOOL. But only two are good. Which two?

73 Fill in the square so that all three rows from left to right and all three columns from top to bottom form valid three-letter words.

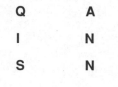

```
Q       A
I       N
S       N
```

74 Can you find the nine-timer on the board below? Your rack is HIORTWZ.

| 3W | | | 2L | | | E₁ | 3W |

75 Put two letters after TWELVE to make an eight-letter word.

76 Talking of twelve, why does twelve plus one equal eleven plus two?

77 Many common names, including those below, are allowable Scrabble words. Can you match the words to the meanings?

COLIN	A billiards shot.
ERIC	A small Genoese coin.
PETER	A butterfly.
JANE	A quail.
JENNY	A prison cell.
VANESSA	A fine paid by a murderer.

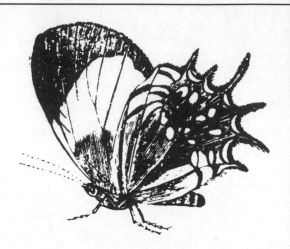

78 Can you get one word from the letters DOWNROE?

79 KEP means `to catch', SAR means `to savour', FLEME means `to put to flight' and SPAE means `to foretell'. Which one of the following is allowed, and what's wrong with the other three?

KEPPED, SARRED, FLEMED, SPAED.

80 What letter precedes MELINITE to make a nine-letter word?

81 That fabled Scrabble beast, the twenty-seven-timer, is mentioned elsewhere in this book. Now's your chance to make one. Your rack is AGHILMP and the board looks like this.

| 3W | | | 2L | | | E₁ | 3W |

82 OSW contains about 130,000 words. The most common initial letter is S. Approximately how many words begin with S? (a) 6,700 (b) 8,700 (c) 10,700.

83 And what are the next three most common initial letters?

84 What can you do to the words AT, IS, UEY and UEYS, and no other words?

85 You have seen how `hooking' – putting one letter before or after a word to make a

longer word – can help you to make bonus plays. Can you find:
(a) nine hooks to put before ITCH
(b) eight hooks to put after CUR
(c) five hooks for HOOK

86 Which one of the following is a valid word?

PHS, TAS, UMS, XUS.

87 Find two common eight-letter words, one meaning `sweets' and the other meaning `worried', which are palindromes of each other.

88 Starting with the nine-letter word as shown, remove one letter at a time and shuffle the letters to obtain an eight-letter word, then a seven, and so on down to two. Some letters are already filled in to give you a start. There is more than one answer.

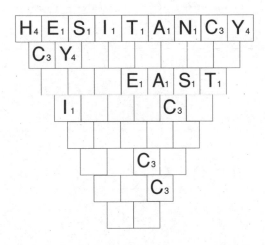

89 What letter does the blank represent on the board below?

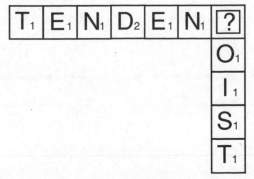

90 You may not have heard of these seven-letter words, but they all have a common anagram. Can you find them?

ANAPEST, BERTHES, FLANEUR.

91 And the same for these eight-letter words:

TROUVERE, DIEBACKS, CINEREAL.

92 For this question, we are considering only words whose second letters come after their first in the alphabet. For each initial letter, what is the first word alphabetically to come into this category? So, for A, you need the first word beginning AB, which is ABA. For B, there being no words beginning BC, the answer is BDELLIUM. How many can you fill in from C to X? (Don't bother looking for a Y, nor, obviously, a Z.)

93 Which one of these is not an allowable word?

FROUFROU, CARACARA, GREEGREE, DIVIDIVI.

94 What common four-letter word can mean: a colour; a small ship; a chaffinch; a minnow; a yellow lake; to wink; to knock; to serrate an edge?

95 Find the nine-timer on the board below. Your rack is EIMOORV.

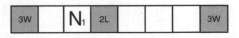

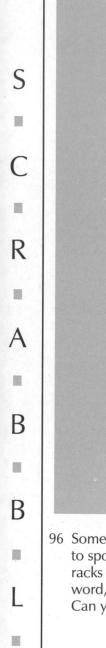

S
C
R
A
B
B
L
E

SOLITAR, INSTOAT, ASTEISE, TUGSAIR.

97 Starting with the nine-letter word QUARTZIER, remove one letter at a time, this time without shuffling the letters, to obtain an eight-letter word, then a seven, and so on down to two.

98 Fill in the square so that all three rows from left to right and all three columns from top to bottom form valid three-letter words.

G		V
A		I
L		A

99. **All of these have a common nine-letter anagram. Can you spot them?**

MAIDSTONE, TADCASTER, MINNESOTA.

100. **What letter does the blank represent on the board below?**

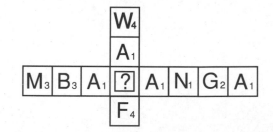

96 Some common words seem unusually hard to spot on a Scrabble rack. The following racks all make an everyday seven-letter word, but have defeated expert players. Can you do better?

THE RECORD BREAKERS

S
C
R
A
B
B
L
E

Highest individual game score

With the emphasis for most of the top players turning to matchplay in recent years, high-scoring games are seldom a feature of competitive Scrabble. However, in more relaxed mood high scores are still achieved and in 1989 Phil Appleby, one of the UK's most prolific Scrabble players, broke through the 1000–point barrier in a friendly game he played against his sister, Gilli.

Recalling it in *Onwords*, Phil described it like this:

There were three significant phases in the game. The first was when, holding GILQRU? I considered the possibility of the nine-timer LACQUERS. I played off GI and picked up AS. Easy game, Scrabble.

The second was when, holding DEIORSZ I opened the nine-timer by playing the E onto FOR. In any other game I'd have taken the 63 points on offer for ZEA, ZO, but I just felt like gambling. I immediately picked up the X, and realized that if I made ER at the bottom of the board and picked up an I, I

could play OXIDIZERS for a very large score (assuming it was a word). Two moves later I discovered it was.

The third phase involved my pickups after OXIDIZERS. When I immediately found a blank on my rack I thought a third nine-timer around the D of BIRD was my best chance of a record score. Yet there were still plenty of tiles in the bag. After fishing for one go I decided instead to play my bonus, followed it with a second, and prayed that Gilli couldn't go out. She couldn't, I had a nice scoring rack, and suddenly my score was over 1000.

The whole game took about forty minutes; there was no tile tracking, no deep thought. Obviously I was helped by Gilli's disallowed words and unlucky pickups, but then again any record score relies on one's opponent having an unlucky game. It all seemed so straightforward. Next week, 1100?

This is how the game progressed.

	A	B	C	D	E	F	G	H	I	J	K	L	M	N	O
1	3W			2L	N₁	A₁	V₄	E₁				2L			3W
2		2W					H₄	I₁		3L				2W	
3			2W		D₂	A₁	S₁	T₁	A₁	R₁	D₂		C₃		
4	2L		A₁	G₂	O₁			2L			B₃	I₁	R₁	D₂
5				E₁	L₁	M₃					P₃	O₁	T₁		
6		P₃	E₁	L₁	L₁	3L					B₃	A₁	Y₄	3L	
7		E₁	F₄			2L		K₅	O₁	W₄	S₁	2L			
8	L₁	A₁		2L		N₁	O₁	V₄	A₁			2L			3W
9	A₁		2L				Y₄		M₃	E₁	W₄	2L			
10	C₃	O₁	T₁	E₁	R₁	I₁	E₁			H₄	I₁	N₁		J₈	
11	Q₁₀				2W	T₁					N₁			E₁	
12	U₁			2W			2L				G₂	I₁	F₄	T₁	2L
13	E*		T₁	O₁	U₁	R*	I₁	N₁	G₂			O₁	E₁		
14	R₁	U₁	E₁			3L				3L			R₁	2W	
15	S₁		E₁	A₁	U₁		O₁	X₈	I₁	D₂	I₁	Z₁₀	E₁	R₁	S₁

122

Highest score for a single move

Karl Khoshnaw, runner-up to Allan Saldanha in the 1993 National Scrabble Championship, is also the holder of the record for the highest score for a single move in a genuine game of Scrabble, an astonishing 392 points! This he achieved on 11 April 1982. His rack at the time held the letters ACEIQSU and he was looking to play CAIQUES. Then his opponent innocently opened up two triple-word score squares with a Z between them. This let Dr Khoshnaw play CAZIQUES for 342 points plus a fifty-point bonus. CAZIQUES, incidentally, is the plural of CAZIQUE, a variant spelling of CACIQUE, a West Indian chief.

	A	B	C	D	E	F	G	H	I	J	K	L	M	N	O
1	3W			2L				3W				2L			3W
2		2W				3L				3L				2W	
3			2W				2L		2L				2W		
4	2L			2W				2L				2W			2L
5					2W				F_4		2W				
6		3L				3L			Y_4	A_1	M_3		3L		
7			2L			O_1	2L		W_4	E_1	D_2	2L			
8	3W			2L		I_1	O_1	T_1	A_1		E_1	2L			3W
9			2L			L_1	2L	A_1	X_8	E_1	D_2	2L			
10		3L				B_3			H_4	3L				3L	
11					2W	O_1	D_2				2W				
12	2L			2W		C_3	O_1	U_1	P_3	L_1	E_1	D_2			2L
13			2W				O_1	H_4					2W		
14		2W				3L		I_1		3L				2W	
15	3W			2L		C_3	A_1	Z_{10}	I_1	Q_{10}	U_1	E_1	S_1		3W

The final scores in the game by no means shamed Dr Khoshnaw's opponent, Miss Elizabeth McLymont, who managed 485 to the record breaking lecturer's 697, producing an aggregate score of 1182, which was no small total either.

Highest one-tile score

In May 1983 *Word Ways*, The Journal of Recreational Linguistics*, published the results of Kyle Corbin's study of the highest scores for playing from one to seven tiles in a Scrabble move.

From playing one tile he calculated it would be possible to score 231 points, by adding S to HYDROXYBENZENE and QUICKSILVERING. Eight moves were required to position the tiles correctly before the singles could be played. Those moves were:

1. SNOW
2. SNOWBALL
3. SILVER
4. SILVERING
5. QUICKSILVERING
6. ERG
7. BENZENE, EN, RE
8. HYDROXYBENZENE

The addition of the S to make QUICKSILVERINGS and HYDROXYBENZENES scored 231 points.

	A	B	C	D	E	F	G	H	I	J	K	L	M	N	O
1	3W			2L				3W				2L			Q_{10}
2		2W				3L				3L				2W	U_1
3			2W				2L		2L				2W		I_1
4	2L			2W				2L				2W			C_3
5					2W						2W				K_5
6		3L				3L				3L				3L	S_1
7			2L				2L		2L				2L		I_1
8	3W			2L				S_1	N_1	O_1	W_4	B_3	A_1	L_1	L_1
9			2L				2L		2L				2L		V_4
10		3L				3L				3L				3L	E_1
11					2W						2W				R_1
12	2L			2W				2L				2W			I_1
13			2W				2L		2L				2W		N_1
14		2W				3L				3L			E_1	R_1	G_2
15	H_4	Y_4	D_2	R_1	O_1	X_8	Y_4	B_3	E_1	N_1	Z_{10}	E_1	N_1	E_1	3W

*Word Ways is edited and published by Ross Eckler, Spring Valley Road, Morristown, New Jersey 07960, USA.

S C R A B B L E

Lowest game score

In contrast to the superlative scores mentioned above, *Onwords* asked its readers in July 1981 to come up with the lowest idealized game score, using all 100 tiles. Capitalized words were permissible and Mike Lean managed to come up with a score of only 217.

He achieved it with these inspired moves:

1. OU (the O is a blank)
2. GLABROUS
3. EXPLODE
4. TAKE
5. WHITEN
6. LANE
7. FILTHY
8. OMITTER
9. AGITATE
10. ADZE
11. SEREIN
12. EURO
13. WOOING
14. JUDAISM (the A is a blank)
15. TENABLE
16. CLOACAL
17. AIA
18. LOVE
19. QUERPO
20. ENVIOUS
21. RYFE
22. SOARED

Record bonus game

In 1989 two of the top players in Nottingham achieved a remarkable feat during a game of Scrabble. Russell Byers, whose letter analysis and tips on game improvement came earlier and Shiela Spate, whose husband Clive was runner-up to Mike Willis the 1994 National Scrabble Championship, managed to play ten bonus moves in the course of one game. This had only been recorded twice before. But what set their feat apart was that seven of these bonuses came from consecutive moves!

Russell went first, playing OY. Shiela played LA. Then the seven-move sequence started:

Russell Byers   Shiela Spate

SHINIERANEARING/ALY/NOY

HAPTERONBATEMENT

OVERUSESCREAMED

CLOSURES

When the game ended only twenty-six points separated the players, with Shiela Spate winning 539–513, which shows that not only bonus moves are capable of generating huge scores.

The board looked like this at the end of the game.

Left board

	A	B	C	D	E	F	G	H	I	J	K	L	M	N	O
1	3W	W_4	H_1	I_1	T_1	E_1	N_1	3W	F_4	I_1	L_1	T_1	H_4	Y_4	3W
2	S_1	2W			A_1	3L				3L	A_1			2W	S_1
3	O_1		2W		K_5		2L	G_2	2L		N_1		2W		E_1
4	A_1			2W	E_1	X_8	P_3	L_1	O_1	D_2	E_1	2W			R_1
5	R_1	Y_4	F_4	E_1	2W			A_1			2W	A_1	D_2	Z_{10}	E_1
6	E_1	3L		N_1		3L		B_3		3L		G_2		3L	I_1
7	D_2		2L	V_4		T_1	2L	R_1	2L			I_1	2L		N_1
8	3W			I_1		E_1		O^*M_3	I_1	T_1	T_1	E_1	R_1	3W	
9			2L	O_1		N_1	2L	U_1	2L			A_1	2L		W_4
10		3L		J_8	U_1	D_2	A^*	I_1	S_1	M_3	3L		T_1	3L	O_1
11				S_1	2W	B_3					2W	E_1	U_1	R_1	O_1
12	2L			2W	C_3	L_1	O_1	A_1	C_3	A_1	L_1	2W			I_1
13			2W		E_1	2L	I_1	2L		O_1		2W		N_1
14		2W			3L		A_1		3L	V_4			2W	G_2
15	3W			2L			3W	Q_{10}	U_1	E_1	R_1	P_3	O_1	3W

Right board

	A	B	C	D	E	F	G	H	I	J	K	L	M	N	O
1	3W			2L		A_1	S_1	T_1	E_1	R_1	O_1	I_1	D_2		3W
2		2W		H_4	O_1	W_4			I_1					2W	
3			F_4	A_1	W_4		2L	P_3	I_1	T_1	I_1	F_4	U_1	L_1	
4	2L			P_3				U_1				Y_4			2L
5		B_3	A_1	T_1	E_1	M_3	E_1	N_1	T_1		B_3				
6	C_3	3L		E_1		3L		O_1	V_4	E_1	R^*	U_1	S_1	E_1	E_1
7	L_1		2L	R_1		A_1	L_1	A_1	R_1				2L	C_3	
8	O_1			L_1	O_1		N_1	O_1	Y_4			J_8	E_1	R_1	K_5
9	S_1	H_4	I_1	N_1	I_1	E_1	R_1		2L			Z_{10}	O_1	2L	E_1
10	U_1	3L			A_1				3L		3L		G_2		A_1
11	R^*			2W	R_1					2W				M_3
12	E_1		2W		I_1		Q_{10}			2W			E_1	X_8
13	S_1		2W		N_1	2L	A_1	2L			O_1	D_2
14		2W		N_1	E_1	G_2	A_1	T_1	I_1	N_1	G_2		D_2	2W
15	3W			2L			3W				2L	D_2	I_1	T_1

Highest seven-tile score

Four years before Kyle Corbin's record tile-scores were published, *Word Ways* had carried the seven-tile record devised by the New Zealand player, Jeff Grant. Where Kyle Corbin had restricted his scores to words found in just one dictionary, *Webster's Third New International Dictionary*. Jeff Grant had looked at the possibility of using words from other authoritative sources. As a result he was able to come up with a score of 1,962 points for the playing of seven letters.

In this he was following the 1,961–point score devised by the British players Darryl Francis and Ron Jerome, which had previously appeared in *Word Ways* in May 1974.

To prepare the board for the top-scoring move, Jeff Grant worked out that twenty-eight moves were required. They are:

1 ER
2 SQUANDER
3 ODD
4 OOT
5 DU, TUE
6 TRI, DUT
7 SQUANDERMANIA
8 IM, FA, UN, LI, LA, DUTIFUL
9 ELAT
10 EX, OX
11 AMP, TA
12 GOYIM (the Y is a blank)
13 GAUDE
14 IE
15 IN, EN
16 ODEA (the D is a blank)
17 PROVER
18 AITTS
19 EEVN, ES
20 VAGABOND
21 VAGABONDAGE
22 WIN
23 LEEDS, WE, IE
24 FLOWERET
25 TIEW
26 IO
27 RICKSHAW, AR, BI, OC, WINK, AH, GA
28 JINNYRICKSHAW, AN, GY

Now comes the record move which uses the seven letters: B, Z, Y, C, H, R and S:

29 BENZOXYCAMPHORS, PROVERB, GAUDEZ, DUTIFULLY, SQUANDERMANIAC, FLOWERETH, VAGABONDER, JINNYRICKSHAWS

	A	B	C	D	E	F	G	H	I	J	K	L	M	N	O
1	3W			2L				3W			2L				3W
2		2W				3L		S₁		3L			2W		J₈
3			2W				2L	Q₁₀	2L				2W		I₁
4	2L			2W				U₁			E₁	E₁		V₄	N₁
5					2W			A₁	I₁	T₁	T₁	S₁		A₁	N₁
6		3L				O₁		N₁		3L			G₂		Y₄
7			2L			O₁	D₂	D₂	2L			F₄	2L	A₁	R₁
8	3W			2L		T₁	U₁	E₁				L₁		B₃	I₁
9	P₃		2L				T₁	R₁	I₁			O₁	2L	O₁	C₃
10	R₁	3L		G₂	O₁	Y*	I₁	M₃		3L		W₄	I₁	N₁	K₅
11	O₁	D*	E₁	A₁	2W	F₄	A₁				L₁	E₁	E₁	D₂	S₁
12	V₄			U₁			U₁	N₁				R₁		A₁	H₄
13	E₁		2W	D₂			L₁	I₁	2L			E₁	2W	G₂	A₁
14	R₁	2W	I₁	E₁		E₁	L₁	A₁	T₁	3L		T₁	I₁	E₁	W₄
15	3W	E₁	N₁	2L	O₁	X₈	3W	A₁	M₃	P₃	2L	O₁			3W

125

SCRABBLE® marathon

In March 1995 Paul Golder and John Howell of the Romford Scrabble Club staged a twenty-four hour Scrabble marathon to raise money for Mencap. The event took place at the offices of BBC Radio Essex where Mike Hill, one of the presenters, kept listeners informed of the progress of the match.

Playing fast and open games Paul and John managed to clock up 124 games in the time available, amassing a total of 111,154 points, an average of very nearly 900 points per game.

The photograph shows the final minute of their twenty-four hours. Both players are still going strong. Paul Golder on the right reaches for the bag of tiles while being interviewed by Mike Hill; John Howell is still able to concentrate on his rack.

As Scrabble records go, this must surely be the most physically demanding.

Un-**S**$_1$**C**$_3$**R**$_1$**A**$_1$**B**$_3$**B**$_3$**L**$_1$**E**$_1$® & Co.

UN-SCRABBLE® & Co.

Although the great majority of Scrabble players play the game as it was first devised, there are a number of variations which offer amusing alternatives to the standard game that have been developed over the years.

Some represent minor modifications to the official rules of play, which come under the general category of House Rules. Providing all the players agree in advance to any modifications to the official rules, the introduction of House Rules lets you tailor a Scrabble game to suit the circumstances in which it is being played and the ability of the players. Typical House Rules might include:

Using more than seven letters on your rack.

Setting a limit to the number of times a player may exchange tiles.

Exchanging a blank which has been played for the letter tile it represents.

Allowing the scoring of premiums whenever a premium space is used again.

Setting a time limit for each move a player makes to prevent a game being dragged out by unnecessary pondering.

Having a very short time limit per move, twenty seconds perhaps. This can produce a fun, quickie game of Scrabble to occupy, say, a quarter of an hour.

Allowing the use of proper names, which is barred by the official rules.

Restricting words played to a particular theme. Travel for example, in which PLANE, PASSPORT, CUSTOM, CAR and TOURIST would all be applicable.

In addition to modifications of the official rules, the Scrabble board and other equipment opens up the opportunity to play a variety of distinctly different games such as the ones described below.

Solitaire SCRABBLE®

Alfred Butts, Jim Brunot and the rest of the pioneers of Scrabble may have conceived it as a game for two, three or four players, but they didn't ignore the fact that it can also be an absorbing solo game.

You can play Solitaire Scrabble by drawing seven tiles from a well-shuffled pool and then forming a word in the usual way. When this is scored, the number of letters required to make up the rack to its usual complement of seven are drawn and the second word is formed, just as it would be in a standard game. At the end of the game you can see how your score compares with those from earlier games.

An alternative method of play is to try to get the highest possible score at every move. Once a move has been played, put your remaining tiles back in the pool, mix them up well and take seven new letters before making your next move. In this version the chances of a 50-point bonus are significantly reduced. The only way in which you can score a bonus is if you happen to draw seven tiles that form a word.

One version of Solitaire Scrabble that has endless appeal is trying to achieve the highest possible score, as the previous records show. To do this you deliberately select tiles from a pool that is turned right side up. You use a dictionary as well. As the official rules state `The highest score obtainable in Scrabble is still a mystery' and a lot of players have a lot of fun trying to unravel that mystery as well as raising their own scores.

Duplicate SCRABBLE®

Of all the variants Duplicate Scrabble is probably the most widely played. This is due in part to the popularity of Duplicate Scrabble in France and the rest of the French-speaking, Scrabble-playing world, where the standard game is hardly ever played.

Duplicate Scrabble was invented by a Belgian, Hyppolite Wouters and it differs from the standard game in a number of significant ways:

Any number of players can take part from solo players to several hundred in a tournament.

All the players play with the same tiles, but only receive credit for the words they form.

There is an impartial gamesmaster, or referee, to draw the tiles and decide whether or not to change tiles. By the end of a game every player will have used all, or very nearly all the tiles, of which the French Scrabble set has 102.

As you will appreciate, luck plays no part in Duplicate Scrabble.

At the start of a game each player is seated in front of his or her own board. Everyone has a set of tiles, arranged face up in alphabetical order. Players also have a sheet of paper on which to write down the words they form and the score awarded for those words. They also have a pack of around thirty slips of paper marked with the number each one has been given by the referee.

The referee starts play by drawing seven tiles at random and announcing these to the players. They each take these same tiles from their own sets and try to form the highest possible score with the rack. After two and a half minutes the referee calls that thirty seconds remain for the move and that all words must be written down. Each player writes on one of the slips the word he or she has formed, its score and the grid reference of the first letter of the word. (With horizontal words the number is written first e.g. 9M; for vertical words the letter is written first e.g. M9). When the thirty seconds is up the referee calls for all slips to be handed in and goes round collecting them.

Once the slips have been checked, the referee announces the highest-scoring word and its location on the board. All the players position this word on their own boards (taking away the word they played themselves if it is different). In the case of inadmissible words a player scores nothing.

Should only one player achieve the maximum score in French-speaking Duplicate Scrabble, and providing there are at least sixteen players

taking part, that player scores an additional bonus of 10 points.

Play starts again with the referee drawing tiles to bring the number on the rack up to seven. In the first fifteen racks drawn, there must be a minimum of two vowels and two consonants. From the sixteenth rack onwards there must be a minimum of one vowel and one consonant; blanks count as either vowel or consonant. If a draw of tiles fails to produce this balance, all the tiles are returned and seven new tiles drawn.

The players now have another three minutes to form the highest-scoring word and place it on the board, linking it with the first word, cross-word fashion, as in the standard game of Scrabble. At the end of that move the second word is written on the second slip of paper and handed to the referee for adjudication.

The game continues like this until all the tiles have been drawn, or all the consonants or all the vowels have been played. Players build up their cumulative scores, with the one who has the highest total obviously winning. In cases where two or more solutions achieve the same score, the referee selects the word he or she thinks will best further the game, perhaps by providing the most open board or the best rack.

Although Duplicate Scrabble has the advantage of eliminating the luck factor, it has the disadvantage of not testing several elements of the game, such as all the points of board management and rack management which are so important to top players in the `real' game. It is in fact much more a test of raw word power, with no tactical or strategic element. In theory, the most skilful player will always win, because every player is always faced with the same board and the same rack of tiles.

Duplicate is also probably a less sociable game than the standard game. The post-game discussion between players of who did what right or wrong is one of the most enjoyable aspects of Scrabble. By its very nature this is virtually lost in Duplicate.

SCRABBLE

SCRABBLE® Bingo

Scrabble Bingo is much like ordinary Bingo but played with Scrabble tiles. It also shares certain similarities with Duplicate Scrabble.

A game starts with each player writing down two seven-letter words, making sure that in the two words they do not use more of any one letter than there are in the Scrabble set.

Letters are then called out, just like the numbers in Bingo, and players strike out the ones in their words as they hear them. As soon as all the letters of both words have been crossed through, a player calls `Scrabble Bingo' and hands over his or her words to be checked.

Players may only cross through one letter at a time, so that if your two words contain three Is, the letter I has to be called three times before they are all crossed through.

Binary SCRABBLE®

Binary Scrabble is a game for two players which was devised by John Bowness formerly secretary of Leicester Scrabble Club. It is based on the principle that both players know in advance what their tiles will be throughout the game.

To begin with fifty tiles are drawn at random for each player and the two sequences are written down.

The game follows the official rules of Scrabble with these modifications:

Players are allowed to change tiles as often as they wish, the exchanged tiles being placed at the end of their sequence of fifty in the order in which they were picked up.

Play ends when one player has played all of his or her tiles. The sum of the opponent's remaining tiles is deducted from his or her score, but it is not added to the total of the player who has `gone out'.

The two sets of fifty letters are designated Player A and Player B. Player A always goes first and the two players will always play two games, so that each has a turn with Player A's

letters and Player B's letters. Players are allowed to record where they have reached by marking the place on lists of letters, but they are not allowed to write down a record of their opponent's letters; for this they must rely on memory.

Blank Option SCRABBLE®

David Gibson, one of the leading American players has invented a variant which reduces the luck element in Scrabble. In his version each player is given a blank to play at any stage in the game. After drawing six tiles each turn, a player can choose to draw a seventh tile or take the blank, which remains on the rack until it is played, thereby ensuring that players can plan to maximize the benefit of a blank tile.

Super-SCRABBLE®

Super-Scrabble was invented by another top American Scrabble player Nick Ballard, publisher of the Scrabble magazine *Medleys*.

As the name suggests Super-Scrabble is really a game of Scrabble on a larger scale, played to more or less the same rules but on a twenty-five by twenty-five board in place of the standard fifteen by fifteen one.

The board has a number of other differences. In addition to the familiar premium squares: double-letter (2L), triple-letter (3L), double-word (2W) and triple-word (3W), there are super premium squares: quadruple-letter (4L), quintuple-letter (5L), quadruple-word (4W) and quintuple-word (5W).

The Super-Scrabble board also has Chameleon letter squares (CL) and Chameleon word squares (CW). They mimic the last premium square covered by either player, by assuming the same value as that square. To show Chameleon squares at work, Nick Ballard gives the example of a player opening with a word that covers a double-letter square and a double-word square. In this instance the Chameleon letter square is worth 2 (mimicking the double-letter square) and the Chameleon

1	2	3	4	5	6	7	8	9	10	11	12	13	14	15	16	17	18	19	20	21	22	23	24	25
5W				2L				3W				3L				3W				2L				5W
	4W				3L				2W						2W				3L				4W	
		4W				2L				5L				5L				2L				4W		
			3W				3L				4L		4L				3L				3W			
2L				3W				2L				CW				2L				3W				2L
	3L				2W				CL						CL				2W				3L	
		2L				2W				4L				4L				2W				2L		
			3L				2W				3L		3L				2W				3L			
3W				2L				2W				2L				2W				2L				3W
	2W				CL				2W						2W				CL				2W	
		5L				4L				3L				3L				4L				5L		
			4L				3L				2L		2L				3L				4L			
3L				CW				2L				2W				2L				CW				3L
			4L				3L				2L		2L				3L				4L			
		5L				4L				3L				3L				4L				5L		
	2W				CL				2W						2W				CL				2W	
3W				2L				2W				2L				2W				2L				3W
			3L				2W				3L		3L				2W				3L			
		2L				2W				4L				4L				2W				2L		
	3L				2W				CL						CL				2W				3L	
2L				3W				2L				CW				2L				3W				2L
			3W				3L				4L		4L				3L				3W			
		4W				2L				5L				5L				2L				4W		
	4W				3L				2W						2W				3L				4W	
5W				2L				3W				3L				3W				2L				5W

word square is also worth 2, mimicking the double-word square. If a second player then covers a triple-letter square on the next move, the Chameleon letter square is worth 3 for the next turn, but the Chameleon word square would continue to be worth 2 since nothing caused it to change.

The Super-Scrabble board above shows the layout of the squares which can be copied by anyone wanting to make a board of their own. Nick Ballard suggests colouring the squares like this:

32 X Double-letter squares (2L) – light blue

32 X Triple-letter squares (3L) – dark blue

16 X Quadruple-letter squares (4L) – light green

8 X Quintuple-letter squares (5L) – dark green

8 X Chameleon-letter squares (CL) – yellow

29 X Double-word squares (2W) – pink

16 X Triple-word squares (3W) – red

8 X Quadruple-word squares (4W) – purple

4 X Quintuple-word squares (5W) – black

4 X Chameleon-word squares (CW) – orange

To get the feel of Super-Scrabble he suggests starting with a standard set of 100 Scrabble tiles, playing according to the official rules of

Scrabble as you get used to the variety of premium squares on the Super-Scrabble board.

Once you have the hang of the principles you will be ready to move to using two sets of tiles, either mixed together, or one bag of tiles in one colour for one player and a second bag of tiles in a different colour for the second player.

Next comes what Nick Ballard describes as the `Preparatory' stage in which two different coloured sets of tiles are used with two racks for each player. Each player begins with seven tiles on each of his or her two racks. At each turn a player is allowed to play, or exchange, one to seven tiles from one of his or her racks, replenishing the rack with tiles of the same colour.

Beyond this lies `Super-Scrabble proper' which uses three different-coloured sets of tiles and three racks per player.

A game of Super-Scrabble ends when the bag is empty and the last of the tiles of that colour are played. The player achieving this `out-play' receives a bonus amounting to double the point-count value of his or her opponent's rack. Play then continues, whether the other bags are empty or not, with whatever sets of tiles remain.

Super-Scrabble offers new areas of strategy when it comes to setting yourself up for bonus plays. You can keep a promising rack `on ice', playing your other two racks until the letter you are waiting for is drawn to make your bonus word. That, the additional premium squares and the Chameleon squares, make Super-Scrabble a game of wide-ranging possibilities, amply rewarding the time taken in learning and board preparation.

Clabbers

Nick Ballard is also the inventor of Clabbers (the name gives a clue as to how this works).

Played on a standard Scrabble board, or Super-Scrabble board, Clabbers allows players to play any combination of letters providing the letters played form an anagram of an acceptable Scrabble word and as long as the arrangement of letters they are joined to on the board also forms an acceptable Scrabble word.

Un-SCRABBLE®

Once a standard game of Scrabble has ended, but before the tiles are removed from the board, you might enjoy a quick game of Un-Scrabble, which as its name suggests consists of removing tiles from the board.

The winner of the standard game usually begins, with any number of players taking it in turns to follow. Each player takes at least and not more than six letters from the board in a go, following these rules:

The tiles removed in each turn must be taken from one word still remaining on the board, though not necessarily from adjacent squares.

After each player's turn, all the tiles remaining on the board must form complete words which are properly interconnected with all the other words.

Play ends when all the tiles have been removed from the board or when it is impossible to continue without breaking the rules.

There are two ways of scoring in Un-Scrabble:

Letter tiles may be counted at their face value points as they are removed from the board, with the player scoring the highest total winning the game.

Alternatively the tiles can be counted at their values modified by the premium squares from which they are removed. Double-letter-score and triple-letter-score squares apply to the letters removed from them; and double-word-score squares and triple-word-score squares apply to the total value of the letters removed in the move in which the premium square is revealed. The player with the highest total score at the end of the game wins. ❑

Alfred Butts openly admitted his bewilderment at the popularity of Scrabble but by the time he died he was able to see Scrabble played around the world, and presumably around the clock somewhere on the globe.

He was also able to see Scrabble as the world's best selling word game, with 100 million sets having been sold in thirty-one different languages in over 100 countries. He could see Scrabble played by post, played on television, and on the point of being played on the Internet. Scrabble clubs were well established in all the major playing countries as were national tournaments and the World Scrabble Championship.

The Language of SCRABBLE®

In 1995 the number of languages in which Scrabble is manufactured passed the thirty mark with the inclusion of Croatian, and Slovenian, producing a language list like this:

Afrikaans	English	Malaysian
Arabic	Finnish	Norwegian
Braille	Flemish	Polish
Catalan	French	Portuguese
Chinese	German	Russian
English	Greek	Slovak
Croatian	Hebrew	Slovenian
Cypriot	Hungarian	Spanish
Greek	Icelandic	Swedish
Czech	Italian	Turkish
Danish	Japanese	
Dutch	English	

Even relatively familiar languages like French and German have sets of Scrabble tiles that differ from the English language set. French Scrabble has 102 letters and although German Scrabble has 100 (including four blanks), the 'Y' has a point value of 10 and players each have eight tiles on their racks, not the familiar seven tiles most of us are used to.

When it comes to languages with different alphabets designing a Scrabble set becomes even more complex. Take Russian for example. In a Russian set there are thirty-three different tiles, as well as blanks, and a total of 104 tiles.

Hungarian might be said to occupy the middle ground; it uses the Roman alphabet but the use of those letters is very different to their English usage. When it came to creating Hungarian

The World of SCRABBLE®

If you find yourself in any of these countries you'll never be without Scrabble. Even if you've left your travelling set behind, you'll find a set on sale somewhere. Though you may find the language something of a challenge.

Afghanistan	British Virgin	Dominican	Iceland	Mexico	Russia	Tobago
Algeria	Islands	Republic	India	Mongolia	Saudi Arabia	Togo
Andorra	Brunei	Ecuador	Indonesia	Morocco	Seychelles	Trinidad
Angola	Burma	Egypt	Iran	Nepal	Sierra Leone	Tunisia
Argentina	Cameroon	Falkland	Ireland	Netherlands	Singapore	Turkey
Australia	Canada	Islands	Israel	New Zealand	Slovak	
Austria	Chad	Fiji	Italy	Niger	Republic	Uganda
Bahamas	Channel	Finland	Jamaica	Nigeria	Slovenia	USA
Bahrain	Islands	France	Japan	Norway	South Africa	Venezuela
Bangladesh	Chile	Gabon	Jordan	Oman	Spain	Vietnam
Barbados	China	Gambia	Kenya	Pakistan	Sri Lanka	
Belgium	Costa Rica	Germany	Korea	Panama	Sudan	Western
Belize	Côte d'Ivoire	Gibralta	Kuwait	Peru	Sweden	Samoa
Benin	Croatia	Greece	Lebanon	Philippines	Switzerland	Zaire
Bermuda	Cyprus	Haiti	Luxembourg	Poland	Syria	Zambia
Bolivia	Czech	Honduras	Malaysia	Portugal	Taiwan	Zimbabwe.
Brazil	Republic	Hong Kong	Malta	Qatar	Tanzania	
	Denmark	Hungary	Mauritius	Romania	Thailand	

Scrabble Spears contacted a professor of Hungarian at the School of Slavonic and East European Studies at London University who agreed to work on the distribution of tiles for the Hungarian letter set. Hungarian has a number of letters which appear infrequently and the ratio of vowels to consonants is quite different to English. Calculating a letter set for Scrabble is not simply a case of looking at letter frequencies. The type of words allowable and playable in Scrabble also need to be taken into account; so must the sort of scores which should be achievable.

After several attempts an acceptable Hungarian version of Scrabble was devised and when this was sent to Hungary, where an unofficial version had been available, the official version from Spears proved to be more popular.

A further month was needed for a skilled engraver to make the steel tool used to print the Hungarian letters, a process which from start to finish had taken six months and which resulted in this set of tiles.

SCRABBLE® on the Internet

Computer Scrabble has been popular for some time and the development of the Internet opens up the possibility for interactive games worldwide via modem, telephone lines and satellites.

A prime mover in this field is the Australian Scrabble Players Association (ASPA) and in particular John Holgate whose ideas on developing a Scrabble vocabulary were featured earlier. Using the World Wide Web (WWW) the ASPA has created what John describes as `a gateway to a "virtual" Scrabble Club'. The WWW he succinctly describes as `a global network of documents and databases linked electronically. Individuals and organizations create "home pages" giving access to information, games and software on over three million computers. By clicking on links you are immediately taken to related documents and databases around the world.'

The ASPA Electronic Scrabble Club offers a number of items from the Menu:

1 Scrabble Trivia Quiz, which poses a wide range of questions like what was Alfred Butts's middle name?

2 Frequently Asked Questions (FAQs – pronounced `facks') – all you need to know about Scrabble. Compiled by Steven Alexander at Berkeley University in California, this amounts to a mini-encyclopedia on the game and provides links to all the Scrabble-related resources on the Internet. Using FAQs it is possible to order books and software, visit other clubs or browse a library of articles on Scrabble.

3 The Club Room where you can have a social game or chat with other players. Both this and the Tournament Room (below) give access to interactive games via TELNET to the `server computer' in Toronto.

4 The Tournament Room in which you can play in a tournament or watch a game in progress.

5 The Scrabble Hall of Fame – portrait gallery, records room, annotated games.

6 The ASPA Notice Board – details of ASPA activities.

7 Tile Talk – an online magazine with Scrabble news from around the globe, puzzles, information on how to build your Scrabble vocabulary and access to online word lists.

To play Scrabble on the Internet players call up one of three DOOMs (Distributed Object Oriented Mud), which is a `networked textual reality' designed by a group of Scrabble players at the University of Toronto. There are currently three DOOM servers available, two for social and `public' games and one for expert players. Players can choose the dictionary they want to use. The computer records the score and the time played, and the matches are rated.

Scrabble on the Internet is growing in popularity with 2000 games a month played on the Toronto servers in which many of the leading US tournament players take part. This level of activity is set to expand as other national Scrabble bodies, like the ASPA, develop programmes of their own. For those who relish a taste of international Scrabble without having to go out of the front door Scrabble on the Internet opens up promising new horizons.

SCRABBLE® Clubs

Since March 1993 I have been managing Scrabble Clubs UK which has given me the chance to get to know the Scrabble club Movement inside out and appreciate its growth and development. The first Scrabble Club, the London Scrabble League (LSL) was formed in 1971. By 1980 it had been joined by about forty others around the country. By the time I took over at Spears from Leonard Hodge numbers had risen to 219 and two years on Scrabble Clubs UK had just under 300 clubs registered with it, though there were additional unregistered clubs.

In 1993 I organized the first Schools Under-16 Scrabble Championships. Two years later the School Club mailing list numbered 362 with a further 200 clubs entering for the 1995 Championships.

Of the adult clubs, just over a third are active in the organizing and playing of Scrabble competitively. The largest club, the London Scrabble League, has around 170 members; the average club size is eighteen and holds meetings once a fortnight. This gives over 5000 players meeting regularly for a game of Scrabble, of whom perhaps 750 compete in

tournaments other than those at their own clubs.

As part of the continuing expansion of Scrabble clubs *Scrabble Club News* is published bi-monthly to provide news and information to club members or individual readers interested in Scrabble. For subscription details please write to me:

> Philip Nelkon
> Scrabble Clubs UK
> Richard House
> Enstone Road
> Enfield
> Middlesex
> EN3 7TB

I would be very pleased to hear from you.

Postal SCRABBLE® Club (PSC)

Since 1973 it has been possible to play Scrabble by post thanks to the Postal Scrabble Club and its hard-working officers. Although the PSC no longer organizes events, back in 1981 the first PSC Scrabble weekend tournament was held in Leamington Spa when forty players took part. Today the PSC provides an invaluable service for enthusiasts who, for any number of reasons, are unable to attend Scrabble Clubs. The free use of the dictionary in PSC games also helps less experienced players establish a good Scrabble vocabulary for face-to-face games.

Details about the Postal Scrabble Club and its newsletter may be obtained from:

> Debbie Williams
> 3 Oak Close
> Moreton
> Wirral
> L46 OUH

Onwords

Onwords started life in July 1980 as *Onwards on words* (a title which lasted for just one issue) as a means of providing postal Scrabble players with information about league tables, finished games and Scrabble in general. Such information had previously appeared as one of several games covered by the magazine of the National Games Club, *Dolchstoss*. Since this appeared irregularly and contained much that was of little interest to Scrabble players, *Onwords* provided a publication devoted entirely to Scrabble and one that it was hoped would appeal to players beyond those engaged in postal Scrabble.

Allan Simmons has edited and published every issue since its inception and has had the satisfaction of seeing *Onwords* become established as the definitive magazine for keen Scrabble players in the UK, with a readership extending to all the major Scrabble playing countries around the world. As such it provides a forum for authoritative correspondence and discussion on all aspects of the game. It carries articles by leading players on strategy and words (some of which appear in this book). It covers all the major national and international Scrabble tournaments. It also carries annotated games like the ones already featured here as well as Scrabble puzzles, cartoons and items of general amusement to anyone who enjoys playing Scrabble.

Subscription details may be obtained from the
> Editor and Publisher:
> Allan Simmons
> Shilling House
> 1 Woolmer Hill
> Haslemere
> Surrey
> GU27 1LT

The Association of Premier Scrabble Players (APSP)

The Association of Premier Scrabble Players was established in 1987. The statement announcing its formation described that its main aims would be 'To promote the playing of Scrabble to a matchplay (i.e. play to win) format, to organize cash prize tournaments, and to seek substantial sponsorship for such events.' Since then it has done a great deal to promote matchplay Scrabble, starting with the British Matchplay Scrabble Championship which was inaugurated in the APSP's first year. As the editor's note in *Onwords* made clear,

when the formation of the APSP was announced, 'the APSP is an association to unite all Scrabble players and is not just designed to satisfy the needs of the top players. Use of 'Premier' in the title is not intended to indicate that the Association is only for top players, more to distinguish it as a premier organization for all competitive Scrabble enthusiasts.'

Details about APSP can be obtained from:
> Gareth Williams
> 209 Fidlas Road
> Llanishen
> Cardiff
> South Glamorgan
> CF4 5NA

National SCRABBLE® Championships

The National Scrabble Championship will be twenty-five years old in 1996. In that time it has seen many changes but still retains its position as the premier UK Scrabble tournament.

Since 1989 the NSC has been played to a matchplay format. In 1994 the final was held over three days with all sixty-six contestants playing nine games. At this point the top four players played a round robin of a further three games, carrying their scores forward from round 9. On the last day the top two players after twelve rounds played a final constituting the best of five games to find the Champion. The deciding game of this Championship was one of the four annotated games which came earlier in the book and the winner, Mike Willis, was rewarded with a leather bound copy of *The Chambers Dictionary*, a gold-plated Scrabble set from Franklin Mint and a Royal Doulton vase; his victory also guaranteed him a place in the 1995 World Championships.

World SCRABBLE® Championships

In the autumn of 1990 J.W. Spear & Sons PLC announced that they would be generously

National SCRABBLE® Championships

S
C
R
A
B
B
L
E

Head-to-head competition in the preliminary rounds.

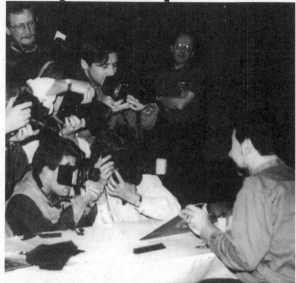

The 1994 National Scrabble Champion, Mike Willis, meets the press.

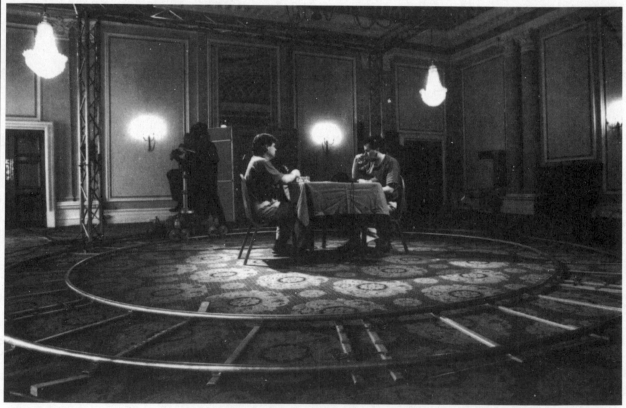

Head-to-head in the finals while the closed circuit television cameras relay the match to the audience in an adjacent room.

Every rack and move is scrutinized and evaluated by the audience following the games on the giant TV monitor and Scrabble board.

The 1992 champion receives the winner's prizes. The three others pictured with me are all key figures in the world of Scrabble. From left to right they are: Francis Spear the Chairman of J.W. Spear & Sons PLC, Catherine Schwarz the editor of *The Chambers Dictionary* and Gyles Brandreth who founded the championship and who has acted as a commentator at many of the finals.

sponsoring the first World Scrabble Championships in London in September 1991. Forty-eight qualifiers from countries where English Scrabble is played would be competing for prizes ranging from $500 for the fifth-placed player to $10,000 for the World Champion.

Twenty-one countries were invited to take part and the competitors came from all walks of life and spanned all ages. Allan Saldhana, one of the eight members of the UK team, was almost fifty years younger than the most senior competitor. There was a chef from Bahrain, a coin dealer from South Africa, an auditor from Japan, a music professor from Canada and a logologist from New Zealand.

The international flavour of the event was enhanced by the acceptance of both British and American spelling. *Official Scrabble Words* (1990) and *The Official Scrabble Players Dictionary* (1978) acted as the definitive reference works, so players not familiar with one or the other had a lot cramming to do as they hastily added unfamiliar but potentially vital words to their vocabularies; longer words not covered by either of these were checked in the two adjudicators' dictionaries *The Chambers Dictionary* (1988) and *Webster's 9th New Collegiate Dictionary*.

BBC2 covered two of the semi-final games and the three games of the final. Alan Coren presented these with Darryl Francis, one of the most knowledgeable authorities on the game, providing a learned commentary on each move and its strategic possibilities.

In the end the North American players triumphed with three American players and one Canadian contesting the semi-finals. After an all-American final between Brian Cappelletto (aged twenty-two) and Peter Morris (seven years his senior), Peter Morris won the match and became the first World Scrabble Champion. An English graduate student from Michigan State University, he had been US National Champion in 1989 and had been rated among the top five Scrabble players in the USA for eight years.

As you will have gathered from the earlier annotated game, the second World Championships held in New York in September 1993 saw a UK victory, with Mark Nyman winning a thrilling final match to restore British pride. The British team as a whole had a much more satisfactory championships than two years earlier.

The 1995 World Championships (once again in London), had sixty-four players from the widest spread of countries so far. Based on performances in the 1993 WSC and the wish to include as many countries as possible the distribution of invitees was:

Mark Nyman (reigning champion) 1

Naween Fernando (reigning Gulf Champion) 1

Australia 4	Bahrain 1	Canada 5
Eire 1	France 1	Ghana 2
Hong Kong 1	Iraq 1	Israel 2
Japan 1	Kenya 2	Kurdistan 1
Kuwait 1	Malaysia 1	Malta 1
Nigeria 3	New Zealand 4	Pakistan 1
Philippines 1	Saudi Arabia 1	Seychelles 1
Singapore 1	South Africa 2	Sri Lanka 1
Trinidad 1	UAE 1	UK 10
	USA 10	

After fifteen games, the top four players were to be separated to play an extra three games against each other, carrying forward their scores from the first fifteen games. The top two after eighteen rounds would contest the Final.

In the same way the next four were to be separated to play each other for fifth, sixth, seventh and eighth positions, the same for ninth, tenth, eleventh and twelfth and so on.

As in previous World Championships both the latest edition of OSW and OSPD were to be used as were Tournament tiles, special Scrabble tiles without indentations which ensure total fairness when they are picked from the bag. ❑

SCRABBLE CHALLENGES

CONSONANT PLAY – ANSWERS

1 VICTRIX
2 HOWEVER
3 JACUZZI
4 FLUMMOX
5 WHIPSAW
6 DWARVES
7 QUARTZY
8 VANDYKE
9 XIPHOID
10 YASHMAK
11 MIDWIFE
12 KILLJOY
13 FLYOVER
14 DOWNBOW
15 NEPHEWS
16 PEEVISH
17 TZADDIQ
18 JAYWALK
18 POLYZOA
20 VEHICLE
21 BOXFULS
22 NETWORK
23 LOCKJAW
24 GATEAUX
25 HOATZIN
26 LOBIPED
27 FIREBOX
28 WOODWAX
29 JACKDAW
30 WORKSHY
31 BEZIQUE
32 CUMQUAT
33 PICKAXE
34 JAZZMAN/MEN
35 SIXFOLD
36 WAXWORK
37 CADENZA
38 MAJESTY
39 BOXWOOD
40 DEEJAYS

THE TWO-BLANK CHALLENGE

ONE ANSWER

1 EQUINOX
2 SHOWBIZ
3 HYMNARY
4 FRECKLY
5 TWITCHY
6 IJTIHAD
7 TUGHRIK
8 DVANDVA
9 ORIFICE
10 WHORISH
11 KNOWHOW

12 MEGOHMS
13 UNFROCK
14 ASSISTS
15 BETWIXT
16 FULCRUM
17 GAZEBOS
18 SYNONYM
19 ZOCCOLO
20 CAVEMAN
21 GALLFLY
22 SIXTHLY
23 PAJAMAS
24 WYSIWYG
25 NECKLET
26 VAMPISH
27 OBLOQUY
28 UNSCREW
29 EXHUMED
30 COBWEBS
31 KIBBUTZ
32 KILLJOY
33 FUGUIST
34 OUTJUMP
35 PHLEGMY

TWO ANSWERS

1 CUMULUS, TUMULUS
2 FREEBEE, REFEREE
3 APOPLEX, PERPLEX
4 DOYLEYS, ODYSSEY
5 WARWOLF, WERWOLF
6 HALFWIT, TWELFTH

7 BACILLI, ICEBALL
8 AUCUBAS, SUBAQUA
9 JOYLESS, SOOJEYS
10 AQUAVIT, QIVIUTS
11 DOGWOOD, GODHOOD
12 GAZOOKA, ORGANZA
13 AZIMUTH, SHIATZU
14 MATZOTH, TIMOTHY

THREE ANSWERS

1 AVOCADO, OCTAVOS, VOLCANO
2 ASPHYXY, HYPOXIA, PHARYNX
3 GERKHIN, SKREIGH, SKRIEGH
4 FITCHEW, TWELFTH, WHIFFET

FOUR ANSWERS

1 ZOOGONY, ZOOLOGY, ZOONOMY, ZOOTOMY
2 GROWTHS, WARTHOG, WRIGHTS, WROUGHT
3 DOULEIA, EULOGIA, MOINEAU, SEQUOIA

OUT IN TWO MOVES

1 OVUM, WUS
2 INIA, AIA
3 DZHO, PUP
4 CIAO, AUK
5 WYNN, TYG
6 LULL, OIL
7 SQUIZ, JO
8 DODO, CWM
9 YOUNG, OU
10 TAHA, AHA
11 PACY, SUQ
12 WAHOO, OE
13 PIPI, UTU
14 JAZY, KEX
15 JOKY, ZAX
16 CIVIL, AI
17 NEMN, GYP
18 VIZY, GAP
19 RICH, VLY
20 EPEE, UTU
21 JOKEY, AA
22 AERIE, BI
23 THYMY, CH
24 MICE, EYE
25 VOULU, GI
26 VACUA, CH
27 BRRR, GAY
28 VIVE, NTH
29 OLIO, OIL
30 FIVE, AYU
31 NAVY, IVY
32 ZOOEA, XI
33 IBEX, VLY
34 HIYA, YOU
35 SEXT, EBB
36 WIFIE, IF
37 FECK, LAV
38 BEVY, TWP
39 BAFT, JAK
40 VIBS, PRY

BACKWORDS – ANSWERS

The answers given below are by no means exhaustive, but most of the commonest words up to nine letters long are given. You may well have come up with some perfectly valid answers not listed here.

1 ANTIPASTO, ARISTO, IMPASTO, MANIFESTO, PRESTO
2 BONSPIEL, COCKATIEL, MATERIEL, SCHLEMIEL, SHLEMIEL, SPANIEL, STANIEL
3 DORHAWK, GOSHAWK, MOHAWK, MOLLYMAWK, SQUAWK
4 APOPLEX, COMPLEX, DEFLEX, DUPLEX, MULTIPLEX, PERPLEX, REFLEX, RETROFLEX, SIMPLEX, TRIPLEX
5 CURFEW, FEVERFEW, FLAMFEW
6 LEGITIM, LITERATIM, SERIATIM, SHITTIM, VERBATIM, VICTIM
7 AEROBUS, ARQUEBUS, AUTOBUS, COLUBUS, HELIBUS, IAMBUS, INCUBUS, MINIBUS, NIMBUS, OMNIBUS, RAILBUS, RHOMBUS, SUCCUBUS, SYLLABUS, THROMBUS
8 OVERTAX, SUPERTAX, SURTAX, SYNTAX
9 BRECHAM, BROUGHAM, DIRHAM, FULHAM, GINGHAM, PELHAM, PETERSHAM, SEALYHAM
10 DISTICH, DREICH, ENRICH, FETICH, OSTRICH, QUAICH, SANDWICH, SUPERRICH, TSAREVICH
11 FOREPLAN, GAMELAN, GOLLAN, ORTOLAN, POLLAN, PORTOLAN, RAGLAN, REPLAN, RUBELLAN
12 HETERODOX, ORTHODOX, PARADOX
13 BASHAW, CASHAW, CUMSHAW, HEEHAW, HERNSHAW, KICKSHAW, OAKENSHAW, RICKSHAW, SCRIMSHAW, TRISHAW, UNTHAW, WAPENSHAW
14 CANTERLOO, GARDYLOO, HALLALOO, HALLOO, JORDELOO, SUPERLOO, VINDALOO
15 NAUSEA, OVERSEA, UNDERSEA
16 BRONZE, QUINZE, SCHANZE, STANZE
17 BAMBOO, BOOBOO, BUGABOO, HUBBUBOO, PEEKABOO
18 BLUECAP, ETTERCAP, FOOLSCAP, HANDICAP, MADCAP, NIGHTCAP, SNOWCAP, TOECAP, WHITECAP
19 CRACKJAW, LOCKJAW, STICKJAW
20 CROSSBAR, FOOTBAR, HANDLEBAR, KILOBAR, MEGABAR, MICROBAR, MILLIBAR

21 CERATODUS, EXODUS, FUNDUS, GRADUS, RHABDUS, SOLIDUS

22 BELDAM, COMMENDAM, GODDAM, GRANDAM, MACADAM, MUQADDAM, QUIDAM

23 BANDOLERO, CABALLERO, CAMPANERO, CAVALIERO, PADERERO, PATERERO, PEDERERO, SOMBRERO

24 CASTRATO, INAMORATO, LITERATO, MODERATO, OBBLIGATO, PIZZICATO, POTATO, SFORZATO, STACCATO, TOMATO

25 ACCUSTOM, BOTTOM, CHRISTOM, CUSTOM, DIATOM, PHANTOM, SUBATOM, SYMPTOM

26 ASWARM, BECHARM, DISARM, ENCHARM, LUKEWARM, OVERARM, STRONGARM, UNDERARM, UPSWARM

27 BECLOUD, ENCLOUD, ENSHROUD, INSHROUD, MISPROUD, OVERCLOUD, OVERPROUD, SHROUD, STROUD, UNCLOUD

28 ANTENNA, BANDANNA, DUENNA, FEISEANNA, GOANNA, HOSANNA, PLATANNA, SAVANNA, SIENNA, THANNA

29 AEROBOMB, APLOMB, CATACOMB, COCKSCOMB, COXCOMB, DISENTOMB, ENTOMB, HECATOMB, HONEYCOMB, TOOTHCOMB

30 AMORETTO, ANNATTO, BLOTTO, CORNETTO, DUETTO, FALSETTO, GHETTO, GROTTO, LIBRETTO, MULATTO, NONETTO, RISOTTO, STILETTO, VAPORETTO, ZUCHETTO

31 BEHOWL, GAREFOWL, MOORFOWL, PEAFOWL, UNCOWL, WATERFOWL

32 BONANZA, CADENZA, CREDENZA, INFLUENZA, NYANZA, ORGANZA, STANZA

33 BACKSPIN, BREASTPIN, DRIFTPIN, FIVEPIN, GALOPIN, HAIRPIN, HATPIN, INCHPIN, LINCHPIN, NINEPIN, OVERSPIN, PIPPIN, TERRAPIN, TOPSPIN, UNDERPIN

34 BETRIM, INTERIM, MACHZORIM, MEGRIM, PILGRIM, RETRIM, UNTRIM

35 ALCOHOL, CATECHOL, GASAHOL, GASOHOL, MENTHOL, NAPHTHOL, SEGHOL

36 ANTEFIX, CRUCIFIX, PREFIX, SUFFIX, TRANSFIX

37 BEDOUIN, HARLEQUIN, HENEQUIN, MANNEQUIN, PALANQUIN, PENGUIN, PINGUIN, RAMEQUIN, SAGOUIN, SEQUIN

38 CONCERTO, ESPARTO, HITHERTO, QUARTO

39 ALOOFLY, BARFLY, BLOWFLY, BLUFFLY, BRIEFLY, CATCHFLY, CHIEFLY, CORNFLY, DROPFLY, FIREFLY, FRITFLY, GADFLY, GOUTFLY, GRAYFLY, GREENFLY, GRUFFLY, HORSEFLY, LADYFLY, OVERFLY, STIFFLY

40 BILIRUBIN, BOBBIN, DOBBIN, DUBBIN, DUMPBIN, DUSTBIN, GLOBIN.

41 ANTHELIX, ANTIHELIX, BOLLIX, PROLIX, SPONDULIX

42 COLOPHON, MARATHON, POLYPHON, SIPHON, SYPHON, TALKATHON, TELETHON, WALKATHON

43 IMPETIGO, INDIGO, LENTIGO, VERTIGO, WENDIGO

44 BEDBUG, DOODLEBUG, FIREBUG, HUMBUG, JITTERBUG, LADYBUG

45 MISPICKEL, NICKEL, PANNIKEL, SHEKEL, SNORKEL

46 COCKATOO, GENTOO, TATTOO

47 BLOWGUN, HANDGUN, OUTGUN, SHOGUN, SHOTGUN, UNBEGUN

48 BUTTERCUP, EGGCUP, GILCUP, GILTCUP, HICCUP, KINGCUP, TEACUP

49 BACKSAW, CHAINSAW, FORESAW, FRETSAW, HANDSAW, JIGSAW, SEESAW

50 AMALGAM, CRYPTOGAM, LINGAM, PHENOGAM, POLYGAM, WHANGAM.

51 CROSSBOW, DOWNBOW, LONGBOW, RAINBOW, STEELBOW, SUNBOW

52 BERGAMASK, DAMASK, DISMASK, IMMASKUNMASK.

53 CONTEXT, HYPERTEXT, PRETEXT, TELETEXT, URTEXT, VIDEOTEXT

54 AUTOCAR, FORECAR, HANDCAR, HORSECAR, MINICAR, RICERCAR, SIDECAR, TURBOCAR

55 CHILIAD, EYELIAD, GWINIAD, GWYNIAD, JEREMIAD, MYRIAD, OLYMPIAD

56 BUCKAROO, GOOROO, JACKAROO, JILLAROO, KANGAROO, POTOROO, SMASHEROO, WALLAROO, WANDEROO

57 BUMBAG, HANDBAG, NOSEBAG, RATBAG, RATTLEBAG, SANDBAG, SCHOOLBAG, SCUMBAG, TOOLBAG, WINDBAG

58 CASHEW, CLERIHEW, ESCHEW, FITCHEW, FORESHEW, NEPHEW

59 OUTJET, PULSEJET, PULSOJET, RAMJET

60 FORESAY, GAINSAY, HEARSAY, MISSAY, SOOTHSAY, UNDERSAY

ANAGRAM ANSWERS

1 MIXTURE
2 HOWEVER
  WHOEVER
3 DONSIER
  INDORSE
  ROSINED
4 CREESED
  DECREES
  RECEDES
  SECEDER
5 DARNELS
  ENLARDS
  LANDERS
  SLANDER
  SNARLED
6 DEPOSIT
  DOPIEST
  PODITES
  POSITED
  SOPITED
  TOPSIDE
7 EASTLIN
  ELASTIN
  ENTAILS
SALIENT
SLAINTE
STANIEL
TENAILS
8 ESPRITS
  PERSIST
  PRIESTS
  SITREPS
  SPRITES
  STIRPES
  STRIPES
  TRIPSES
9 ANGRIES
  EARINGS
  ERASING
  GAINERS
  GRAINES
  REGAINS
  REGINAS
  SEARING
  SERINGA
10 EASTING
  EATINGS
  GAINEST
  GENISTA
  INGATES
  INGESTA
SEATING
TANGIES
TEASING
TSIGANE
11 ARMOURY
12 ALMANAC
13 ANGLIFY
14 AXOLOTL
15 AEROBUS
16 ASOCIAL
17 ARCHERY
18 ALLEGRO
19 ACHIEVE
20 ALOOFLY
21 BICYCLE
22 SCOOTER
23 OMNIBUS
24 BIPLANE
25 BRITZKA
26 TROLLEY
27 CATBOAT
28 BOBSLED
29 TRAMCAR
30 JETFOIL
31 FATWAED
32 ROLLOUT
33 DECAFFS
34 KARAOKE
35 BUMBAGS
36 FOODISM
37 KEYPADS
38 WORKDAY
39 SIZEISM
40 PORKIES
41 ALLSEED
42 VELAMEN
43 TWYFOLD
44 BLOOSME
45 EPIGYNY
46 EPITAXY
47 GRANFER
48 ORECTIC
49 PULWARS
50 EKPWELE
51 BENZINE
52 IODIZED
53 ZOOTYPE
54 LIZARDS
55 HERTZES
56 ZEBRULE
57 GAZETTE
58 ZABTIEH
59 ZESTFUL
60 ZEUXITE

S
C
R
A
B
B
L
E

143

SCRABBLE PUZZLES

Puzzle Answer #1
LAVENDER scores 167. Obviously you examine the nine-timers first, and it is perhaps the least likely-looking one, fitting your letters around a V, which yields success.

Puzzle Answer #2
KAZOO/STUNK/WO/HO scores 90. The triple-letter/double-word combination, if you have a high-scoring letter, can be a powerful scorer. When the triple-letter scores two ways, as here, you can be on the way to three figures even without a bonus.

Puzzle Answer #3
MAJESTY/CHINA/EVERY/TRICKSY scores a massive 179. Always look for double-double-word opportunities. It goes without saying that a four-timer will beat an equivalent triple-word score. Other possibilities here would be hooking MAJESTY onto S-EXES (155), PITCHER-S (161), or above and parallel to JUMART starting above the U (163).

Puzzle Answer #4
SPECTRA/REQUIEMS/YUP/ME scores 106. When you have a really good rack like this, don't just charge in with the first bonus you see. Look for the highest-scoring place, as long as it doesn't give too good a chance to your opponent. Here, picking up the triple-word score and adding in REQUIEMS and the smaller words outscores other possibilities such as REDACTS/AN/DOR/AWE (top row) for 93, a four-timer through the H such as TEACHERS (98), CASTERS/REQUIEMS/REACTS (103) and REDCOATS/CHUNK (104). SPECTRA fits the bill nicely.

Puzzle Answer #5
LIEUTENANTS/TWEET scores 80, beating the more obvious ENTRANTS. Bonuses can sometimes be played in the unlikeliest places.

Puzzle Answer #6
WHISPERED scores 162. The nine-timer is the nuclear bomb of the Scrabble board, often flattening your opponent even when it is not a bonus. POWERED/PREFERENCE looks good, but trails in with a mere 143.

144

Puzzle Answer #7
CHUNKY scores 64. When you have high-scoring letters on your rack, look to use premium squares to the maximum effect. Other possibilities here would be a lazy AX/XI (52), HYRAX through the A of ERASABLE (54), YORK/YE/OR above and parallel to ONER (56) or DOXY/TOX/NY, from the D of REDDY (63).

Puzzle Answer #9
ZAXES/FIZZ scores 81. Once again, multiple use of the premium squares outscores the simple bonus. RELAXES/OIL/LEAS would give 72, while the more obscure WRAXLES/OIL gets up to 75.

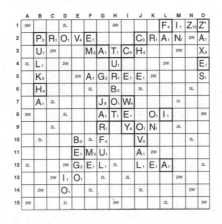

Puzzle Answer #11
QUINTESSENTIAL scores 98, just beating the rather pedestrian INFLATES (94). You will probably never play a fourteen-letter word, but doesn't it look nice?

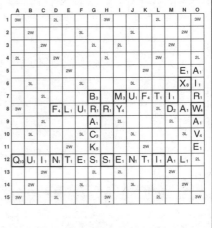

Puzzle Answer #8
METERED/EM/ME/IT/NE/AR/RE scores 92. Fitting a word in like this, with multiple parallel two-letter words, will push the score up – you have twelve extra letters to count. The frustration comes when five of the two-letter words you need exist and the sixth one doesn't!

Puzzle Answer #10
REDNESS/ZAGS scores 122. You may have seen SENDERS first and gone for that in the same place, but a look for the alternative, and not really difficult, seven-letter word from this promising rack yields three extra points. SENDERS/QUIVERS/JOS scores 141, or would do if JOS were a word. The plural of JO is JOES.

Puzzle Answer #12
CAUTION/MAGIC/RESTRAINT/HULLO scores 89. The blank could alternatively be P or N in this position. Other possibilities if you missed the slightly unlikely-looking hooks were ACTIONED onto the D of REVISED (83), or CIBATION through the B of BLAIZE (86).

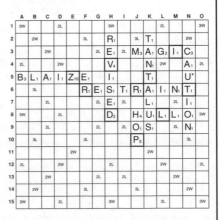

145

Puzzle Answer #13

URBANIZE (88) is the only bonus from this likely-looking rack.

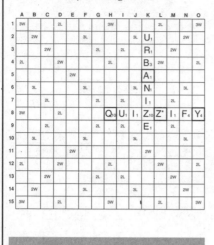

Puzzle Answer #14

PRIMATES, for 62, is the rather disappointing best score. If you made a bonus using JEEP – sorry, the latest edition of *The Chambers Dictionary* gives it a capital letter, so it is not allowed. It was quite valid in previous editions, which meant Scrabble players had to unlearn JEEP when the new edition came into use. Other words have suffered the same fate, such as OP; previously allowed, it is now listed as an abbreviation and therefore invalid for Scrabble. And if you tried a bonus with DJINNIS, that's not allowed either; DJINNI is the plural of DJINN.

Puzzle Answer #15

SCRATCHY/BUZZY scores 158. Y can be a useful letter for hooking – alternative plays here use SAVAGERY, SOLDIERY and even YSLAKED. However, you could only play CATCHY with each of these; only by using the S already on the board can you net a bonus, and a double-double-word into the bargain.

Puzzle Answer #16

RAINDATE scores 86, although ATRAZINE scoring 84 and AERATING for 80 are also good. RETAINA, despite looking like a nice rack, does not make a seven-letter word, and there are precious few places to play one on this board anyway. But you could have had several eight-letter words – CARINATE, MARINATE, DENTARIA, ANTISERA, RESINATA, ARTESIAN, REATTAIN, RABATINE, AERATION, AERATING, and ATRAZINE.

Puzzle Answer #17

VOYAGER/AR scores 60. It's our old friend the double-double-word again, hiding bashfully in that thicket of letters.

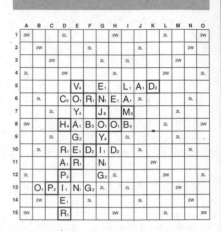

Puzzle Answer #18

TERMINALLY scores 20. At first sight it looks impossible to play anything on this board, but even the most costive of positions will usually provide something if you look hard enough.

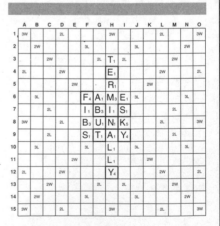

Puzzle Answer #19

You should play TEE (l2d) for 3 points. Knowing what is on the board and what is on your rack, you can work out your opponent's last five letters by simple elimination: BELST. If you play AVOID/BO/LI/AD (a14a) (under and parallel to the BLA of BLASTER), you score 27, but your opponent plays BLEST/GITES (m1d) for 20, he scores 2 and you lose 2 for your remaining tiles, and you lose by 4. By blocking your opponent from playing all his tiles, you make sure you get another shot, playing AVOID as above, or, if your opponent blocks it, AVOID/DA, using the D of MIND.

If you play TEE, your opponent's best move is BELS/TE/EL/GITES (24) (m1d). You then take your 27, your opponent has one point left on his rack, and you grab a one-point win. End-game problems such as this can keep expert players quiet for hours, working out the different possibilities. Now imagine trying it in a real game, with your chess-clock ticking away your last few minutes and the World Championship hanging on whether you get it right. And you thought Scrabble was such a relaxing game!

Puzzle Answer #20

No new move has been placed on the board. The reason for that is there is no `best' move. Let's look at the possibilities.

Yes, you have a bonus. GATHERS/TING scores 69 (j9d), but opens up the possibility of a nine-timer for your opponent. As there are still three tiles in the bag, you do not know what your opponent is holding – but you can work out that he has seven from ABEINOTRY and a blank. These are good letters; by playing GATHERS, you could be giving your opponent, say, BESTIARY. That scores 176, and you've just lost the game. And he didn't even need the blank!

So what else could you do? If your opponent has a bonus, he will have to play it in the same place, using TIN, or by turning QUINTE (h7d) into QUINTES or QUINTET. If you can block both those places, you go a long way to negating his good letters.

TING/GETS (j9d) would be a possibility, or, even better, TINE/ERGS. The three consecutive consonants in ERGS would make it very difficult to play a parallel bonus. Another idea would be QUINTES/STAGER (h13a), forcing him to fit in an eight-letter word – but it's the fear that he can do just that which is stopping you from playing GATHERS in the first place.

You could try playing just two tiles – in that way, even if your opponent plays a bonus, he still has one tile to pick out of the bag, and you get one more turn. But it's hard on this board to play two tiles for any reasonable score.

On balance, heartbreaking though it is to turn down a bonus, I think I would go for the ERGS move. Others may disagree. What it all boils down to is: Do you feel lucky? Well, do you?

SCRABBLE QUIZ ANSWERS

1   K.
2   HEARABLE is not allowed.
3   ALPACA, ARMADA, AZALEA, BANANA, BAZAAR, PANAMA and SALAAM are some of the commonest.
4   SUBZERO, AUGMENT, NUCLEUS.
5   HYDROSKI
6   There are fifteen – ABED, ACE, ACED, BAD, BADE, BEAD, BED, CAB, CAD, CADE, DAB, DACE, DAE, DEB and ECAD.
7   FRANCE is not allowed. (WALES – same as WEALS. SPAIN – to wean. RUSSIA – a type of leather.)
8   FLYWHEEL, EYELINER, PHOTOFIT, POSTCODE.
9   UNSCALED and UNMOUNTED are allowed.
10 PONDWEED.
11 AWARNED, BRAWNED, PRAWNED, REDRAWN, DAWNERS, WANDERS and WARDENS.
    CORACLE, ORACLED, CHOLERA, CHORALE, CALORIE, CARIOLE, COALIER, LORICAE, CAJOLER, EARLOCK, CORELLA, OCELLAR, CAROMEL, CORNEAL, POLACRE, COALERS, ESCOLAR, ORACLES and CALOYER.
    CLAMPER, IMPEARL, LEMPIRA, PALMIER, LAMPERN, PLEROMA, PALMERS, SAMPLER, TEMPLAR, TRAMPLE and LAMPREY.
    DENUDED, UNEDGED, DUDHEEN, UPENDED, ENDURED, DENUDES, DUDEENS and DETUNED.
12 V.
13 DEADLINESS.
14 SHREDDINGS is allowed.
15 SRADDHA (an offer to the spirits of an ancestor), PFENNIG (a German coin), MRIDANG (a two-headed Indian drum), MVULE (an African tree). MULVE also makes VELUM.
16 BEVVY, DIVVY, NAVVY, SAVVY, VALVE, VERVE and VIVID are some of the commonest.
17 There are four: FIG, GHI, GIF, JIG.
18 SIXTE – a type of fencing stroke.
19 UPADAISY, ATTABOY, GERTCHA.
20 O.
21 DANISH is not allowed. (FRENCH – belonging to France, not always capitalized. FLEMISH – to stow a rope in a certain way. DUTCH – a wife.)
22 ALERTED, ALTERED, REDEALT, RELATED, TREADLE.
23 DAIQUIRI.
24 BURPING. Also allowed is UPBRING.
25 BOREDOM. Also allowed is BROOMED.
26 MURDEREE and VISITEE are allowed.
27 NOODLEDOM.
28 MOPED becomes MOPEDS. (Never seen anyone riding a moped?)
29 There are five – KON, MON, MONK, NOM and OLM.
30 CERTAIN, TRAINED, TRAINEE, FAINTER, GRANITE, INGRATE, TEARING, INERTIA, ENTRAIL, LATRINE, RELIANT, MINARET, RAIMENT, PAINTER, PERTAIN, REPAINT, RETRAIN, TERRAIN, TRAINER, NASTIER, RETAINS, RETINAS, NATTIER, NITRATE, URINATE and TAWNIER are some of the commonest.
31 O.
32 GABON is not allowed. (NIGER – a black person. MALI – a gardener in India. ZAIRE – unit of currency in Zaire.)

S C R A B B L E

147

33 SARDANA, BANDARS, CADRANS, CANARDS, ARGANDS, DARSHAN, DHARNAS, RADIANS, MANSARD, RANDANS, PANDARS, NASARDS, ASTRAND and TARANDS. AWARDED, BEDWARD, DWARFED, DAWDLER, DRAWLED and SWARDED. ADVICES, ADVISED, VISAGED, DEVISAL, VIDAMES, INVADES, ADVISER, VARDIES, ADVISES, AVIDEST, DATIVES, VISTAED and SAVVIED.
DORSET combines with eighteen letters to make forty-four seven-letter words. Here are eighteen of them: ROASTED, DEBTORS, ROSETED, DEFROST, STODGER, SHORTED, STEROID, STROKED, OLDSTER, STORMED, RODENTS, ROOSTED, DEPORTS, RODSTER, DETORTS, DETOURS, WORSTED and DESTROY.

34 ADIEU, AERIE, AUDIO, COOEE, EERIE, OUIJA and QUEUE are some of the commonest.

35 WILDE is not allowed. (DICKENS – the devil, as in `what the dickens'. SHAW – a small wood. GILBERT – a unit of force.)

36 TOILETS and LITOTES, the latter meaning `affirmation by negation of the contrary', as in `not inconsiderably'.

37 ASTRINGE.

38 RUSSIAN is not allowed. (WELSH – to renege on a bet. GERMAN – closely related. POLISH – oh, come on.)

39 T.

40 DOURLY is not allowed.

41 There are nineteen – PST, PUR, PURS, PUS, PUT, PUTS, RUST, RUT, RUTS, SPUR, SPURT, SUP, SUQ, SUR, TUP, TUPS, TURPS, UPS and UTS.

42 MARROWSKY – a spoonerism.

43 AIRTIGHT, HAYLOFT, MADWOMAN, GUNFIRE.

44 MALTA is not allowed. (CYPRUS – a thin material like crape. MOROCCO – a type of leather. JORDAN – a chamber-pot.)

45 BOOBOO, COCOON, HOODOO, ROCOCO and VOODOO are some of the commonest.

46 O.

47 TWENTIES, THIRTIES, FORTIES, FIFTIES.

48 GAZEBO.

49 REHEEL and RESOLE are allowed. So is RESTOCKING.

50 STRENGTH.

51 JAPANESE is not allowed. (CHINESE – relating to China, not always capitalized. SIAMESE – to join (e.g. pipes) like Siamese twins. AFGHAN – a heavy knitted blanket or shawl.)

52 PERU is not allowed. (CHILE – a form of CHILD. CANADA – a canyon. JAPAN – a glossy, black varnish.)

53 COTLANDS – lands belonging to a cottage. ENDLANG – on end, ironically a Scottish word.

54 BILANDER, FILANDER, DEARLING, DRAGLINE, HARDLINE, INLANDER and ISLANDER.

55 If you got any, you've beaten the compiler.

56 WORMISH is not allowed.

57 ORLEANS – a type of material. LOANERS is not allowed.

58 I.

59 ZEBRASS – offspring of a male zebra and a female ass.

60 XYSTUS – portico. XERASIA – dry hair. XANTHIC – yellow. XEBEC – boat. XYLOPYROGRAPHY – designs on wood with hot poker. XYSTER – surgical instrument. (Scrabble players' joke: What did one surgeon say to the other? Keep your hands off my xyster.)

61 They can all be preceded by Z.

62 QUAGGA – ass. QUANT – pole. QUASSIA – tree. QUETZAL – bird. QUODLIBET – medley. QUIPU – cords.

63 SJAMBOKS (whips); CTENE (a swimming organ in some sea creatures); AASVOGEL (a vulture); YTTRIUM (a metallic element).

64 TATTOOED.

65 (d)

66 (c)

67 (a)

68 Eight triple-word squares on the board, twelve triple-letters, seventeen double-words, twenty-four double-letters and 164 non-premium squares.

69 MANTEEL (a soldier's cloak or a lady's cape).

70 Women's underclothing.

71 Our suggested answer:

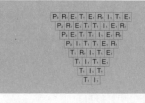

72 LOOPERS and SPOOLER.

73
QUA
INN
SIN

74 HOWITZER.

75 TWELVEMO (a size of paper).

76 TWELVE PLUS ONE is an anagram of ELEVEN PLUS TWO.

77 COLIN – quail. ERIC – murderer's fine, paid to the victim's family. PETER – prison cell. JANE – coin. JENNY – billiards shot. VANESSA – butterfly.

78 Yes – ONE WORD.

79 The past tense of KEP is KEPPIT, of SAR (rhymes with STARE) is SARED, and of FLEME is FLEMIT. SPAED is correct.

80 G.

81 PHANTASMAGORIAL.

82 (c).

83 C (about 7,300), P (about 6,500) and B (about 5,000). Then it's a close-run thing between A, D, M, R and T, all with about 4,600.

84 Put a Q before them.

85 (a) A, B, D, F, H, M, P, T and W. (b) B, D, E, L, N, R, S and T. (c) C and S before, A, S and Y after.

86 PHS.

87 DESSERTS and STRESSED.

88 Our solution is:

```
H E S I T A N C Y
  C Y A N I T E S
  C I N E A S T
  I N S E C T
  C I T E S
  T I C E
  T I C
  I T
```

89 Z.

90 PEASANT, SHERBET, FUNERAL.

91 OVERTURE, BACKSIDE, RELIANCE.

92 CEANOTHUS, DEACON, EF, FIACRE, GHARIAL, HI, IJTIHAD, JNANA, KLANG, LO, MNA, NO, PRAAM, QUA, RUANA, ST, TUAN, UVA, VYING, WYANDOTTE, XYLEM.

93 FROUFROU is not allowed. (CARACARA – a type of hawk. GREEGREE – an African charm. DIVIDIVI – a leguminous plant.)

94 PINK.

95 OMNIVORE.

96 TAILORS, STATION, EASIEST, GUITARS.

97 QUARTZIER, QUARTIER, QUARTER, QUARTE, QUART, QUAT, QAT, AT.

98
GOV
ANI
LEA

99 DOMINATES, CASTRATED, NOMINATES.

100 Q.

Glossary

APSP	Association of Premier Scrabble Players.
ASPA	Australian Scrabble Players Association.
BINGO	An American word for *Bonus*.
BMSC	British Matchplay Scrabble Championships (the major fifteen-game APSP-organized tournament).
BONUS	A word utilizing all seven letters on the rack thus obtaining a 50-point *bonus*.
CHESSCLOCK	A dual-clock (as in chess) for timing games, ensuring equal time for each player.
CLUB KO	The National Scrabble Club Tournament.
COMBINATIONS	Letter groups that fit well with other letters to provide a selection of useful bonus words, memorable because of the common combination.
DOUBLE-CHALLENGE	A rule (not in UK Scrabble) whereby the challenger of a word loses a turn if the challenged word(s) are valid.
DOUBLE-DOUBLE	A word played across two double-word squares to achieve four times the score.
FLOATER	An available letter on the board for playing a word (normally an eight-letter word) through.
GAMESMASTER (GM)	In postal play, the person who umpires the game and deals out the letters to the two players.
HIGHSCORE	A style of play (primarily and more formerly in the UK) where emphasis is to get high scores and high game aggregates rather than winning.
HOOK	A letter added before or after a word to form a valid longer word.
MASTERS	A ten-game highscore event (in UK) for the top forty players each year based on the previous year's highscore tournament averages.
MATCHPLAY	Play-to-win style, as opposed to highscore.
NASC	North American Scrabble Championships.
NATIONAL SCRABBLE CLUB TOURNAMENT	A national Club team tournament played as a straight knockout each year. Loosely and incorrectly known as Club Knockout.
NEUTRALIZING (CHESSCLOCKS)	Pressing the chessclock buttons such that neither clock is going, as required when words are challenged or game disputes arise.
NGC	National Games Club – The postal games club from which the Postal Scrabble Club evolved.
NINE-TIMER	A play across two triple-word squares to achieve nine times the score.
NSC	National Scrabble Championships. An annual event run by J.W. Spear & Sons PLC since 1971 consisting of regional finals and a grand final for those who qualify from the regional finals.
NZASP	New Zealand Association of Scrabble Players.
ONWORDS	*The* Scrabble Enthusiasts' Magazine – published five times a year by Allan Simmons.
OPEN GAMES	In postal play, a game where the sequence of letters is known in advance by both players thus providing more strategic scope.

S	OSPD	*Official Scrabble Players Dictionary* – the Americans' official word authority.
	OSW (jocular OSWald!)	*Official Scrabble Words* – the word authority of the UK Scrabble movement from 1988, based on *The Chambers Dictionary*.
C	PASSING	Forfeiting a turn without playing a word or changing tiles (sometimes voluntarily in the hope that the opponent may provide something useful but also enforced when stuck with unplayable tiles at the end of a game).
	PSC	The Postal Scrabble Club (UK).
R	RACK LEAVE	The letters left on the rack following a play.
	REGIONALS	The regional finals of the National Scrabble Championships (NSC).
	REPLIES	(see STARTS AND REPLIES).
A	SASPA	South African Scrabble Players Association.
	SCRABBLE PLAYERS NEWS	The North American Scrabble *newspaper* for members of their *National Scrabble Association*.
B	SINGLE- CHALLENGE	The challenge rules as used in the UK whereby the challenger does not forfeit a turn for an incorrect challenge – see Double-Challenge.
	SIX-LETTER COMBINATIONS	Groups of six letters often with a high possibility of a seventh letter forming a bonus word (see Combinations.)
B	SPREAD	The difference in points between a winner's and a loser's score represented as a positive number for the winner and a negative number for the loser. Used as a tie-breaker in matchplay.
	STARTS AND REPLIES	Playing first or playing second. At some events there is a system to even out the number of starts/replies for each player.
L	SUM-OF-OPPONENTS' SCORES	The total number of wins a player's opponents had as a measure of the strength of opposition and thereby of use in splitting ties.
	TILE-TRACKING	The recording of tiles played in a game on pencil and paper such that remaining tiles at any point can be determined.
E	TRIPLE-TRIPLE	A word played across two triple-word squares to get nine times the score. Bonus words played thus are affectionately known as NINE-TIMERS.
	TURNOVER	The number of tiles played in a turn.
	WSC	World Scrabble Championships, first held in 1991 for leading players of Srabble in English.

40–739–1